Guide to the 2000 Presidential Election

Guide to the 2000 Presidential Election

Michael L. Goldstein

CQ PRESS

A Division of Congressional Quarterly Inc.
Washington, D.C.

Congressional Quarterly Inc.

Congressional Quarterly Inc., an editorial research service and publishing company, serves clients in the fields of news, education, business, and government. It combines the specific coverage of Congress, government, and politics contained in the *CQ Weekly* with the more general subject range of an affiliated service, the *CQ Researcher*.

Under the CQ Press imprint, Congressional Quarterly publishes a variety of books, including college political science textbooks and public affairs paperbacks on developing issues and events, information directories and reference books on the federal government, national elections, and politics. Among them are the *Guide to the Presidency*, the *Guide to Congress*, the *Guide to the U.S. Supreme Court*, the *Guide to U.S. Elections*, and *Politics in America*. CQ's A-Z Collection is a four-volume reference series that provides essential information about American government and the electoral process. The *CQ Almanac*, a compendium of legislation for one session of Congress, is published each year. *Congress and the Nation*, a record of government for a presidential term, is published every four years.

CQ publishes the *Daily Monitor*, a report on the current and future activities of congressional committees. An online information system, cq.com, provides immediate access to CQ's databases of legislative action, votes, schedules, profiles, and analyses.

CQ Press
A Division of Congressional Quarterly Inc.
1414 22nd St. N.W.
Washington, D.C. 20037

(202) 822-1475; (800) 638-1710

www.cqpress.com

Printed in the United States of America

03 02 01 00 99   5 4 3 2 1

Cover: Debra Naylor, Naylor Design Inc.

Library of Congress Cataloging-in-Publication Data

Goldstein, Michael L., date
   Guide to the 2000 presidential election / Michael L. Goldstein.
      p. cm.
   Includes bibliographical references and index.
   ISBN 1-56802-485-1
   1. Presidents—United States—Election—2000. I. Title.

 JK526 2000
 324.6'3'0973

                                                                99-046808

For Andy Goldstein, age thirteen,
whose pre-campaign has begun on the soccer fields of America

Contents

Tables, Figures, and Boxes

Preface

Although similar to previous editions in general structure, *Guide to the 2000 Presidential Election* reflects two new realities. First, since the initial publication of this series in 1984, the presidential selection process has changed dramatically. Presidential campaigns now span the entire period from one election to the next. The campaign finance system is under scrutiny, but no one has yet figured out how to reform it. The majority of Americans now consider presidential elections not important enough to participate in. A glimpse at the 1984 edition of this book would reveal a stark contrast between what was then and what is now our presidential selection process.

Second, new communications technologies have transformed the way we learn about politics. For educators, this change is especially important because the landscape of our profession, from how we do research to how we teach, has been altered. In particular, the Internet has made almost unlimited materials available to increasing numbers of students of presidential elections. As is characteristic of the Internet, however, these materials have no catalogue or guide, no gatekeeper to distinguish the good from the bad, the credible from the incredible.

This book attempts to deal with both of these new realities through extensive revisions of the previous edition and the addition of new material. Like the other volumes, this edition contains numerous charts and exercises as well as brief profiles of major party, third-party, and independent candidates who may play a role in the 2000 election.

Any review of the current presidential selection process now requires discussion of the lengthy campaign preliminaries and the ever changing role of money and the media. An expanded Chapter 2 and extensive revisions in Chapters 4 and 5 address these issues. Case studies of the precampaign activities of Lamar Alexander, Bill Bradley, and Steve Forbes have been added to Chapter 2; these discussions provide readers with sufficient detail as to how candidates, under the Federal Election Campaign Act, can campaign—without really campaigning—for several years before formally declaring their candidacy.

Preparing a print volume posed the challenge of educating students and general readers in a world that is rapidly moving to the Internet. Although this volume cannot provide click-on access to the burgeoning online materials available about the presidential selection process, it can serve as a print portal to these materials. With this goal in mind, each chapter lists Internet sites of relevance, and the brief profiles of the candidates identify Internet sites about each candidate.

The extensive research and rewriting associated with these changes would not have been possible without the generosity and support of many individuals. Indeed, I have been touched by the wholesale support and cooperation I have received in this endeavor. In particular, I wish to thank Mark Acton, Kevin Murphy, and Catherine Tyrell, Republican National Committee; Herbert Alexander, Emeritus, University of Southern California and Citizens' Research Foundation; Meg Bostrom, Trahan, Burden and Charles; Amy Cody, Oregon Office of the Secretary of State; Steve Duprey, New Hampshire Republican Party; Robert Erikson, University of Houston; Curtis Gans, Committee for the Study of the American Electorate; Paul Hendrie, Center for Responsive Politics; Kelly Huff and Kevin Salley, Federal Election Commission; Gary Langer, ABC News; Philip McNamara and Phil Olaya, Democratic National Committee; Katherine Mountcastle, CBS News; Vincent Nasso, Nielsen Media Research; Lisa Noblin, Texas State Ethics Commission; Richard Noyes, Center for Media and Public Affairs; Lee C. Shapiro, Voter News Service; Martin Wattenberg, University of California at Irvine; and Richard Winger, *Ballot Access News*.

In such efforts, there are also those whose support, encouragement, and general friendship are critical. Again, there are many to whom I am grateful. Melinda Carmen and John Parker cheerfully tolerated my increasing eccentricities at the Claremont McKenna College Washington office as publication day approached. Ambassador Gerald Carmen, former chair of the New Hampshire Republican Party, was always ready to tell me a story from the 1976 and 1980 campaigns, if it would help. It did, and there is at least one recounted in this volume. My assistant, Lisa Gore Seifart, chipped in wherever necessary and never complained, no matter how nonsensical and irrational the task may have appeared. And last, but certainly not least, I want to express my sincere love and appreciation to my family, Susan Bales and Andy Goldstein, for understanding that even a small book may be a great undertaking.

Certainly this book would not have appeared without the support and encouragement of CQ Press. I want especially to thank David Tarr, executive editor, who listened graciously to all my ideas concerning the new version of this book, both good and bad, and Ann Davies, managing editor of textbooks and reference, who improved my sometimes inelegant prose and shepherded this volume through production.

Despite all this wonderful assistance, any errors or omissions are my own.

Guide to the 2000 Presidential Election

Newly declared presidential candidate George W. Bush Jr. and his wife, Laura, face the press—one of the most important actors in the contemporary presidential selection process.

(Source: Jim Bourg, Reuters)

The Changing Political Context

During its first two centuries the United States has weathered a variety of social, economic, and political changes that have influenced the way Americans select their chief executive. Virtually every aspect of the presidential selection process—from who votes to who is elected—has undergone a dramatic transformation.

In the late eighteenth century the United States was newly formed, and many aspects of its political process, including presidential selection, reflected the imperatives of nation building. A small propertied elite that had led the revolt against England established a presidential selection process limited to participation by white propertied males. The process allowed its participants to manage conflict in an expansive new nation by giving them the power to select the top leadership without interference from the majority of Americans.

Suffrage was limited. African Americans in most areas were provided with few rights of citizenship, and women were denied the vote in federal elections and generally in state and local elections as well. In most states additional requirements restricted suffrage to white males who held property of a certain value or paid taxes of a certain amount. Only about 6 percent of the young nation's adult population in 1789 voted for the presidential electors who chose George Washington, and no more than approximately 15 percent of all Americans twenty-one years of age and over were considered qualified to vote in the first presidential elections.

Those who were nominated and those who were elected in this early period accurately reflected the relatively closed nature of the presidential selection process. The first six presidents were members of prominent, upper-class families. Of the twenty-four candidates who received electoral votes in any of the first eight presidential elections, a majority were prominent political figures who had played a role in the American Revolution. Sixty-three percent had attended one of the Continental Congresses.

Much has changed in the presidential selection process since that time. Presidential candidates from the two major parties now are selected at national nominating conventions. Delegates to these conventions are either appointed by the political party or selected by voters in party primaries or caucuses. Other presidential candidates secure a spot on the general election ballot by direct nomination by local voters. The potential electorate includes virtually all citizens eighteen years of age or older—approximately 201 million Americans in November 1998.

The presidential candidates, and their methods for reaching voters, have also changed (see Tables 1-1 and 1-2). Contemporary candidates include the humble, the once humble, and the always wealthy. To campaign among the ever growing electorate, all candidates must spend rapidly escalating sums over increasingly lengthy campaigns. These costs soared to $700 million for all presidential candidates in 1996, compared with $550 million in 1992. The overall rate of increase in campaign spending over the past two decades far outstrips the rising consumer price index and the increase in the number of voters (see Table 1-3).

All that remains of the original presidential selection process is the electoral college. As constitutionally established and as it functions today, the electoral college is the body that actually elects the president. Although the names of electors have been removed from all but a handful of ballots, voters in the 2000 presidential election will still be casting their votes for slates of electors pledged to a presidential candidate. Two hundred years ago electors were chosen by state legislatures or by those limited few who qualified to vote. The framers of the Constitution gave the members of the electoral college considerable leeway in making their selections. Although electors rarely do so, they still may exercise their individual choice for president regardless of the popular vote. Since 1948 seven members of the electoral college have acted in this fashion and become "faithless electors."

Presidential Selection Methods

The contemporary presidential selection process is clearly distinct from the process that existed in the late eighteenth and early nineteenth centuries, but the transformation was neither rapid nor direct. Furthermore, the change in this process is ongoing.

The Constitutional Plan

At least four distinct methods of presidential selection can be identified since the first presidential election in 1789. The first method focused on the electoral college as a deliberative body. States decided how their representatives to the electoral college were to be selected and were apportioned electors equal to their combined total of senators and representatives (a

rule that continues today). Each elector would cast two votes to be divided between two candidates. The deliberations of the college resulted in the selection of a president (the individual receiving the most votes) and a vice president (the individual receiving the second largest vote). If there were a tie or if no candidate received a number of votes equal to a majority of the number of electors, the House of Representatives selected a president from among the top five candidates or from the top two candidates who had tied.

By 1804 this original constitutional plan had been amended. The 1800 election produced a tied electoral vote, caused by confusion over who was a presidential candidate and who was a vice presidential candidate. The House ultimately selected Thomas Jefferson as president, on February 17, 1801. The election prompted adoption of the Twelfth Amendment to the Constitution, which reduced the number of votes that each elector cast to one and separated the balloting for president and for vice president. (This distinction later became meaningless as almost all electors were pledged to voting for a party slate composed of a presidential and vice presidential candidate.) If no candidate for president or vice president received the votes of a majority of electors, the House would select a president or vice president from among the top three candidates.

The Congressional Caucuses

The Twelfth Amendment codified a second presidential selection process that had begun in practice as early as 1800. By that year members of Congress who identified with particular political parties were meeting in caucuses to nominate their party's presidential and vice presidential candidates. Meanwhile, state party leaders were nominating slates of electors pledged to those candidates. By 1824 qualified voters in eighteen of the twenty-four states were voting directly for competing slates of electors.

The congressional caucus system of presidential selection, however, worked only as long as interparty competition demanded intraparty discipline to nominate candidates and to carry on a campaign. With the demise of the Federalist Party by 1816, intraparty competition within the Democratic-Republican Party threatened the caucus system. In 1824 the Democratic-Republican congressional caucus, attended by a minority of the party's congressional delegation, nominated one candidate, while dissenting Democratic-Republicans nominated three other candidates through state legislatures or mass meetings. When none of the candidates received a majority in the electoral college, the House selected the president. The caucus system, long under attack, was thoroughly discredited. By 1840 all major political parties were holding national nominating conventions to select their presidential candidates.

The National Nominating Conventions

The rise of this third electoral method—national nominating conventions—was associated with improved means of transportation and with the rapid democratization of the presidential selection process. Improvements in transportation, which enabled more citizens to attend the conventions, moved at lightning speed. In only one year a trip from New York to Philadelphia was reduced from half a day by steamboat and rail to two hours by rail alone. Concurrently, the decline in voting restrictions for white males and the rise of citizen participation in the selection of presidential electors swelled the ranks of voters. In the election of 1824, the last presidential election in which a congressional caucus selected at least one of the candidates, the popular vote for president totaled fewer than 400,000 votes. In the election of 1840, the first in which all major parties nominated their candidates at a national convention, the total popular vote topped 2.4 million (see Table 1-4). By 1848 all but one state selected presidential electors on the same day, reflecting both the increased popular and national dimensions of the election. In general, these changes suggest the rapid transformation in the first half of the nineteenth century of the presidential selection

In 2000, 100 million

process from a measured debate among sequestered elites to what one of the chants of the new popular politics identified as the "great commotion." Indeed, this period is associated with levels of public participation in politics that far surpass any other in American political history.

The national nominating convention remains a major feature of the political landscape. At national nominating conventions in Los Angeles and Philadelphia, the Democratic and Republican Parties, respectively, will select their 2000 standard-bearers. The convention system that was established by the election of 1840, however, is different from later conventions in several respects.

First, all delegates to the early national nominating conventions were chosen directly by party leaders or at party gatherings. Most delegates to the Democratic and Republican conventions were selected by a state convention, by congressional district conventions, or by both. Delegate selection, with few exceptions, was a matter left to the states or to state parties.

Second, for much of the nineteenth century, the formula for state representation at the conventions was fixed. From 1852 on, delegate representation at the Democratic convention was limited to twice the number of the state's senators and representatives. In 1860 Republicans adopted a comparable rule for state representation at their conventions. No matter what the strength of the party was in a particular state, convention representation was set at four at-large delegates plus two delegates for each congressional district.

The control of delegate selection by party leaders in the early convention years made it difficult, if not counterproductive, for presidential aspirants to make appeals directly to delegates or to the party rank and file. Indeed, until the convention system was altered in the early twentieth century, the sole focus of presidential aspirants and the public was on balloting at the convention. In most cases where no incumbent was running, more than one ballot was needed to nominate a candidate.

Finally, beginning at their first national convention in 1832, Democrats established that two-thirds of all delegate votes would be required to nominate a candidate. This rule essentially made party unity a precondition for nomination and gave minority factions within the party substantial veto power in the nominating process.

The Modified Convention System

The assault on party dominance by progressives and a schism within the Republican Party in 1912 (which led to an unsuccessful third-party candidacy by former president Theodore Roosevelt) were the catalysts to major changes in the presidential nominating conventions of the two major parties. The result was a fourth method of presidential selection—the modified convention system.

In 1905 progressive forces at the state level began passing statutes that established the presidential primary as a direct means for citizens to select delegates to the national nominating conventions. Although presidential primaries were not used in the presidential election of 1908, progressive forces aligned with either former president Roosevelt or Sen. Robert La Follette, R-Wis., suddenly saw them as a convenient way to battle a Republican Party apparatus controlled by President William H. Taft. By 1916 twenty states held presidential primaries, thus establishing this method of delegate selection as a regular feature of the political landscape.

The 1912 schism within the Republican Party also brought to a head the issue of apportionment of delegates to national nominating conventions. Delegates from southern states with few Republican voters had wielded considerable influence in the renomination of President Taft. In the presidential election of 1908 the Democrats had won all ten southern states. In six of these states the Republican popular vote had been less than 30 percent of the total vote cast. Yet at the 1912 Republican convention the ten southern states had 228 delegate votes, more than 21 percent of the total delegate votes.

Virtually all of these southern delegates voted to renominate Taft.

For the 1916 convention Republicans put into effect a new arrangement that gave some recognition to local party strength in the apportionment of delegates. The Democrats adopted comparable rules in 1944. This change was fueled in part by efforts of southern Democrats to recoup the influence lost when the two-thirds nominating rule was replaced in 1940 by a simple majority.

Although the modifications in the presidential nominating conventions did not remove party leaders altogether from participation in the selection of nominees, they did open alternative paths to nomination and bolstered the role of the party rank and file and the public in the nomination process. One alternative route involved new ways of gaining access to the media. Candidates who received attention from the print media and from the rapidly developing electronic media—especially television—could translate this coverage into primary votes and ultimately the nomination. For example, in 1940 and 1952, respectively, presidential candidate Wendell Willkie's close connections with two national periodicals (*Look* and *Fortune*) and Tennessee senator Estes Kefauver's extensive television coverage as chairman of the Senate Organized Crime Investigating Committee bolstered serious challenges to Republican and Democratic party leaders.

Despite the new emphasis on participation by citizens as opposed to that of party leaders, this presidential selection system is characterized by substantially lower levels of public participation than was the previous system. This suggests that parties and partisanship, no matter how corrupted by the turn of the century, may have tied citizens in unique ways to the world of politics and presidential elections.

A New Presidential Selection System?

Reform in delegate selection procedures and ongoing changes in the media have further altered the modified convention system. The role of third-party and independent presidential candidates has increased dramatically. Some observers say changes since 1968 have resulted in an entirely new presidential selection system. And again one correlate of further change has been still lower levels of public participation and interest in the presidential election process.

The 1968 Democratic convention triggered a wave of internal party reforms related to the presidential selection process. In that year the Democrats nominated Vice President Hubert H. Humphrey as their presidential candidate. Humphrey had not formally entered a single primary because the incumbent president, Lyndon B. Johnson, had been in the running. Johnson, however, withdrew unexpectedly from the campaign after the New Hampshire primary. Despite his absence from the primaries, Humphrey nonetheless received 67 percent of the total delegate votes at the convention. As a result, disgruntled Democrats who opposed Humphrey and disagreed with party leadership over a wide variety of domestic and foreign policy issues pushed for sweeping changes in the delegate selection process.

The product of this dissatisfaction was the McGovern-Fraser commission report on delegate selection, which was adopted by the Democratic National Committee in 1971. Changes included abolishing the "unit rule," by which states could require their convention delegation to agree upon one candidate who would receive all of the delegation's votes; requiring the delegate selection process to occur within a specified "window" during the same year as the election; limiting the selection of delegates by state party committees; selecting at least 75 percent of a state's delegates at the congressional district level or below; and requiring affirmative efforts by each state to increase the delegate representation of minorities and women.

Additionally, the national Democratic Party adopted a charter in 1974 that significantly strengthened its power, at the expense of state party influence, to enforce the recent changes and other delegate selection procedures. Further Democratic rule making in 1976

banned winner-take-all and open primaries and mandated that delegates in each state be divided among candidates in proportion to the votes they received in Democratic caucuses or primaries. Finally, in 1980 the national Democratic Party adopted rules requiring all delegations to be equally divided among men and women and stipulating that all delegates selected through primaries or caucuses be officially pledged to a presidential candidate (or officially uncommitted) and for one convention ballot bound to that preference.

These changes produced a fundamentally new type of nominating convention marked by considerable rank-and-file influence in the Democratic delegate selection process and virtually no control over the process by party leaders or elected officials. The number of presidential primaries proliferated under the new rules, and party caucuses became open to mass participation. The immediate result was the selection in the next two elections of two "outsiders," South Dakota senator George McGovern in 1972 and former Georgia governor Jimmy Carter in 1976. Neither would have been likely choices of conventions dominated by party leaders.

One unforeseen consequence of the Democratic Party's new rules was that they produced nominees who were either unelectable or who, if elected, could not govern. In the first three general elections after the adoption of the new rules, Democratic nominees garnered on average only 43 percent of the total vote, and the Democrats' only successful candidate during this period, Jimmy Carter, struggled as president with the legislative wing of his own party. This problem, critics argued, was a product of the exclusion of important elements of the party from the nominating convention. For example, only 14 percent of Democratic senators and 15 percent of Democratic representatives participated as voting delegates at the 1980 Democratic convention. A dozen years earlier, under the previous rules, 68 percent of the Democratic senators and 39 percent of Democratic representatives had participated as delegates.

A related complaint held that the proliferation of primaries forced candidates to start early and to compete for mass support in each state. This situation not only made winning the nomination an expensive exercise in political survival but also opened an increasingly public process to media scrutiny. In this regard, the party was losing control over its own deliberations as the media began to play a major role in the winnowing of candidates. The influence of party leaders in the selection of a nominee was thereby even further diminished.

Stirred by these complaints and a succession of defeated nominees, the Democratic Party moved in the 1980s to balance earlier reforms with efforts to provide the national nominating convention with more freedom from rank-and-file directives. By 1992 a new balance had been established. Substantial elements of earlier reforms remained, including a requirement that all delegations be equally divided between men and women and a ban on all winner-take-all or bonus schemes in the allocation of delegates. The Democratic rule makers additionally maintained a strict time frame, or "window," for all delegate selection events. Democrats moved away from earlier reforms, however, by facilitating the return of party leaders and elected officials to the nominating convention. This was done by creating two new categories of delegates. The first included party and elected officials who would attend the convention by virtue of their elected or appointed positions. These delegates would be pledged to presidential candidates according to the caucus or primary votes of their respective states. The second category, primarily governors and members of Congress and the Democratic National Committee, would also be guaranteed delegate slots but officially would be unpledged. Finally, Democratic rule makers attempted to increase the deliberative potential of conventions by not binding delegates to vote for their original presidential preferences on the first or any subsequent convention ballot.

In sum, the Democratic Party's rules for delegate selection were in constant flux in the 1970s and 1980s, reflecting to a large degree an ongoing struggle for power. In 1992 the election of Bill Clinton and Albert Gore, the Democrat's first successful slate in sixteen years, and the movement of the party to the ideological middle put to rest decades of internal party squabbles over delegate selection. As a result, changes in the rules of delegate selection for the 1996 or 2000 conventions have been minor.

The Republican Party has retained a much more federated structure than the Democratic Party and has generally been loath to adopt delegate selection rules that are binding on state parties. Nonetheless, changes in the Democratic rules have had an effect on Republican procedures. In the 1970s and 1980s Democratic-controlled state legislatures often required Republicans as well as Democrats to conform to new delegate selection procedures, such as scheduling primaries or caucuses. A case in point is the southern regional primary, known as "Super Tuesday," which was created in 1988. Initiated by Democratic-controlled state legislatures to bolster the chances of moderate Democratic presidential candidates, the new schedule of early primaries and caucuses throughout the region also applied to Republicans. Only after making substantial gains in state legislative races in November 1994 did the Republicans regain the ability to control their own delegate selection procedures.

Although reluctant to mandate delegate selection procedures, Republicans have attempted to address the difficult issues of minority and gender representation at their conventions and of the timing of delegate selection. Since 1964 at least three reform commissions have made suggestions on how the party's base could be broadened and the delegate selection process opened to new groups. In 1996, fearful that the race for the nomination had effectively been shortened to no more than six weeks, Republicans instituted an elaborate bonus system, giving extra delegates to states who held primaries or caucuses late in the spring of election year, and established an official window during which all primaries or caucuses must be held.

Third-party or independent presidential candidates also play an increasingly prominent role in the current presidential selection process. The vote for third-party candidates totaled 20 percent in 1992 and almost 10 percent in 1996. As in the 1820s, when the old congressional caucus nominating system was in disrepair but not yet replaced by party nominating conventions, some presidential candidates are now nominated directly by their supporters at the state level. In this regard, nomination at a major party convention is currently only one route to the general election ballot and potentially to the presidency.

The continuing changes in the presidential selection process have been fostered not only by the increasing democratization of American politics but also by technological change. The development of rail transportation, improved roads, popular newspapers, and the telegraph made national nominating conventions and national presidential elections possible. Similarly, the development of mass advertising, first through an independent press and later through radio and television, weakened the ability of political parties to monopolize political communication with voters. In this regard, the latest round of technological change is associated with the decline in support for the two major parties, the rise of candidate-centered rather than party-oriented campaigns, and the increasing ability of third-party or independent presidential candidates to communicate directly with voters.

With the aid of new and sophisticated technology, presidential candidates today communicate with an increasing number of Americans. Not only can candidates reach mass audiences through radio and television but they can target their appeals to smaller and more select populations through direct mail, videotape technology, and the Internet. No less important, however, has been the impact of several decades of technological innovation on the costs of presidential campaigns. Although radio and television are effective means of communicating with voters in an age of weak parties, these media are also expensive. Ironically, the need to raise money to pay for these new forms of communication is a further cost.

The overall result of these changes is that lengthy presidential campaigns, often beginning years before the election, cannot be won without millions of dollars. Despite campaign finance reform designed to level the financial playing field, the Republican and Democratic candidates who have raised the most money have received their party's nomination in every election but one since 1976. Lack of the requisite millions has eliminated many potential candidates of prominence and increasingly has made a run for the presidency feasible for those who can finance a campaign through their personal wealth. Indeed, the 2000 presidential election may be the first since the passage of campaign finance legislation in the 1970s in which a candidate who does not participate in the public funding provisions of the Federal Campaign Finance Act, and therefore runs without expenditure limits, will secure the nomination of one of the major parties. The ultimate irony of two centuries of democratization in presidential selection is that we now have a process that is heavily dependent on the resources of the wealthy and powerful and fails to engage the majority of citizens.

Table 1-1   Backgrounds of U.S. Presidents

President	Age at first political office	First political office	Last political office[a]	Age at becoming president	State of residence[b]	Higher education[c]	Occupation
1. George Washington (1789–1797)	17	County surveyor	Commander in chief	57	Va.	None	Farmer, surveyor
2. John Adams (1797–1801)	39	Surveyor of highways	Vice president	61	Mass.	Harvard	Farmer, lawyer
3. Thomas Jefferson (1801–1809)	26	State legislator	Vice president	58	Va.	William and Mary	Farmer, lawyer
4. James Madison (1809–1817)	25	State legislator	Secretary of state	58	Va.	Princeton	Farmer
5. James Monroe (1817–1825)	24	State legislator	Secretary of state	59	Va.	William and Mary	Farmer, lawyer
6. John Quincy Adams (1825–1829)	27	Minister to Netherlands	Secretary of state	58	Mass.	Harvard	Lawyer
7. Andrew Jackson (1829–1837)	21	Prosecuting attorney	U.S. Senate	62	Tenn.	None	Lawyer
8. Martin Van Buren (1837–1841)	30	Surrogate of county	Vice president	55	N.Y.	None	Lawyer
9. William Henry Harrison (1841)	26	Territorial delegate to Congress	Minister to Colombia	68	Ind.	Hampden-Sydney	Military
10. John Tyler (1841–1845)	21	State legislator	Vice president	51	Va.	William and Mary	Lawyer

President	Age at first office	First political office	Last office before presidency	Age at inauguration	State	Education	Occupation
11. James K. Polk (1845–1849)	28	State legislator	Governor	50	Tenn.	University of North Carolina	Lawyer
12. Zachary Taylor (1849–1850)	—	None	[a]	65	Ky.	None	Military
13. Millard Fillmore (1850–1853)	28	State legislator	Vice president	50	N.Y.	None	Lawyer
14. Franklin Pierce (1853–1857)	25	State legislator	U.S. district attorney	48	N.H.	Bowdoin	Lawyer
15. James Buchanan (1857–1861)	22	Assistant county prosecutor	Minister to Great Britain	65	Pa.	Dickinson	Lawyer
16. Abraham Lincoln (1861–1865)	25	State legislator	U.S. House of Representatives	52	Ill.	None	Lawyer
17. Andrew Johnson (1865–1869)	20	City alderman	Vice president	57	Tenn.	None	Tailor
18. Ulysses S. Grant (1869–1877)	—	None	[a]	47	Ohio	West Point	Military
19. Rutherford B. Hayes (1877–1881)	36	City solicitor	Governor	55	Ohio	Kenyon	Lawyer
20. James A. Garfield (1881)	28	State legislator	U.S. Senate	50	Ohio	Williams	Educator, lawyer
21. Chester Arthur (1881–1885)	31	State engineer	Vice president	51	N.Y.	Union	Lawyer
22. Grover Cleveland (1885–1889)	26	Assistant district attorney	Governor	48	N.Y.	None	Lawyer
23. Benjamin Harrison (1889–1893)	24	City attorney	U.S. Senate	56	Ind.	Miami of Ohio	Lawyer

Continued

Table 1-1   *Continued*

President	Age at first political office	First political office	Last political office[a]	Age at becoming president[b]	State of residence[b]	Higher education[c]	Occupation
24. Grover Cleveland (1893–1897)	26	Assistant district attorney	U.S. president	52	N.Y.	None	Lawyer
25. William McKinley (1897–1901)	26	Prosecuting attorney	Governor	54	Ohio	Allegheny	Lawyer
26. Theodore Roosevelt (1901–1909)	24	State legislator	Vice president	43	N.Y.	Harvard	Lawyer, author
27. William H. Taft (1909–1913)	24	Assistant prosecuting attorney	Secretary of war	52	Ohio	Yale	Lawyer
28. Woodrow Wilson (1913–1921)	54	Governor	Governor	56	N.J.	Princeton	Educator
29. Warren G. Harding (1921–1923)	35	State legislator	U.S. Senate	56	Ohio	Ohio Central	Newspaper editor
30. Calvin Coolidge (1923–1929)	26	City councilman	Vice president	51	Mass.	Amherst	Lawyer
31. Herbert Hoover (1929–1933)	43	Relief and food administrator	Secretary of commerce	55	Calif.	Stanford	Mining engineer
32. Franklin D. Roosevelt (1933–1945)	28	State legislator	Governor	49	N.Y.	Harvard	Lawyer
33. Harry S. Truman (1945–1953)	38	County judge (commissioner)	Vice president	61	Mo.	None	Clerk, store owner

President				State	College	Occupation
34. Dwight D. Eisenhower (1953–1961)	—	None	[a] 63	Kan.	West Point	Military
35. John F. Kennedy (1961–1963)	29	U.S. House of Representatives	U.S. Senate 43	Mass.	Harvard	Newspaper reporter
36. Lyndon B. Johnson (1963–1969)	28	U.S. House of Representatives	Vice president 55	Texas	Southwest Texas State Teacher's College	Educator
37. Richard Nixon (1969–1974)	29	U.S. House of Representatives	Vice president 56	Calif.	Whittier	Lawyer
38. Gerald R. Ford (1974–1977)	36	U.S. House of Representatives	Vice president 61	Mich.	University of Michigan	Lawyer
39. Jimmy Carter (1977–1981)	38	County Board of Education	Governor 52	Ga.	U.S. Naval Academy	Farmer, businessman
40. Ronald Reagan (1981–1989)	55	Governor	Governor 69	Calif.	Eureka	Entertainer
41. George Bush (1989–1993)	42	U.S. House of Representatives	Vice president 64	Texas	Yale	Businessman
42. Bill Clinton (1993–)	31	State attorney general	Governor 46	Ark.	Georgetown	Lawyer

Sources: Norman C. Thomas and Joseph A. Pika, *The Politics of the Presidency*, 4th ed. (Washington, D.C.: CQ Press, 1997), 471–473; and *Presidential Elections, 1789–1996* (Washington, D.C.: Congressional Quarterly, 1997), 8.

[a] This category refers to the last civilian office held before the presidency. Taylor, Grant, and Eisenhower had served as generals before becoming president.
[b] The state identified is the primary residence of the president during his adult years, not necessarily where he was born.
[c] Refers to undergraduate education.

Table 1-2   Presidential Selection: A Historical Review

Election year	Winning candidate	Means of selection
1789	George Washington	Original constitutional plan
1792	George Washington	Original constitutional plan
1796	John Adams	Congressional caucus
1800	Thomas Jefferson	Congressional caucus
1804	Thomas Jefferson	Congressional caucus
1808	James Madison	Congressional caucus
1812	James Madison	Congressional caucus
1816	James Monroe	Congressional caucus
1820	James Monroe	Congressional caucus
1824	John Quincy Adams	State legislatures
1828	Andrew Jackson	State conventions, mass meetings, and state legislatures
1832	Andrew Jackson	National convention
1836	Martin Van Buren	National convention
1840	William Henry Harrison	National convention
1844	James K. Polk	National convention
1848	Zachary Taylor	National convention
1852	Franklin Pierce	National convention
1856	James Buchanan	National convention
1860	Abraham Lincoln	National convention
1864	Abraham Lincoln	National convention
1868	Ulysses S. Grant	National convention
1872	Ulysses S. Grant	National convention
1876	Rutherford B. Hayes	National convention
1880	James A. Garfield	National convention
1884	Grover Cleveland	National convention
1888	Benjamin Harrison	National convention
1892	Grover Cleveland	National convention
1896	William McKinley	National convention
1900	William McKinley	National convention
1904	Theodore Roosevelt	National convention
1908	William H. Taft	National convention
1912	Woodrow Wilson	Modified national convention
1916	Woodrow Wilson	Modified national convention
1920	Warren G. Harding	Modified national convention
1924	Calvin Coolidge	Modified national convention
1928	Herbert Hoover	Modified national convention
1932	Franklin D. Roosevelt	Modified national convention
1936	Franklin D. Roosevelt	Modified national convention
1940	Franklin D. Roosevelt	Modified national convention
1944	Franklin D. Roosevelt	Modified national convention
1948	Harry S. Truman	Modified national convention
1952	Dwight D. Eisenhower	Modified national convention
1956	Dwight D. Eisenhower	Modified national convention
1960	John F. Kennedy	Modified national convention
1964	Lyndon B. Johnson	Modified national convention
1968	Richard Nixon	Modified national convention

Table 1-2　*Continued*

Election year	Winning candidate	Means of selection
1972	Richard Nixon	Modified national convention
1976	Jimmy Carter	Modified national convention
1980	Ronald Reagan	Modified national convention
1984	Ronald Reagan	Modified national convention
1988	George Bush	Modified national convention
1992	Bill Clinton	Modified national convention
1996	Bill Clinton	Modified national convention

Table 1-3　Presidential Spending and Votes, 1960–1996

Year	Actual spending (in millions of dollars)	Adjusted spending (in millions of dollars)	Votes cast (in millions)
1960	30.0	30.0	68.8
1964	60.0	57.3	70.6
1968	100.0	85.1	73.2
1972	138.0	97.7	77.6
1976	160.0	83.2	81.6
1980	275.0	98.9	86.5
1984	325.0	93.7	92.7
1988	500.0	126.5	91.6
1992	550.0	117.8	104.4
1996	700.0	132.1	96.3

Source: Herbert E. Alexander, "Spending in the 1996 Election," in *Financing the 1996 Election,* ed. John Green (Armonk, N.Y.: M. E. Sharpe, 1999).

Note: Adjusted spending is the actual spending corrected for changes in the consumer price index (CPI) since 1960.

Table 1-4   Voter Participation in Presidential Elections

Election year and winning candidate	Population of voting age	Voters	Percentage of voting-age population voting
1828 Andrew Jackson	5,201,000	1,155,000	22.2
1832 Andrew Jackson	5,914,000	1,218,000	20.6
1836 Martin Van Buren	6,710,000	1,505,000	22.4
1840 William Henry Harrison	7,566,000	2,412,000	31.9
1844 James K. Polk	8,840,000	2,701,000	30.6
1848 Zachary Taylor	10,081,000	2,879,000	28.6
1852 Franklin Pierce	11,582,000	3,162,000	27.3
1856 James Buchanan	13,235,000	4,045,000	30.6
1860 Abraham Lincoln	14,880,000	4,690,000	31.5
1864 Abraham Lincoln	16,450,000	4,011,000	24.4
1868 Ulysses S. Grant	18,019,000	5,720,000	31.7
1872 Ulysses S. Grant	20,176,000	6,460,000	32.0
1876 Rutherford B. Hayes	22,724,000	8,422,000	37.1
1880 James A. Garfield	25,462,000	9,217,000	36.2
1884 Grover Cleveland	28,275,000	10,053,000	35.6
1888 Benjamin Harrison	31,377,000	11,383,000	36.3
1892 Grover Cleveland	34,522,000	12,061,000	34.9
1896 William McKinley	37,745,000	13,907,000	36.8
1900 William McKinley	41,077,000	13,968,000	34.0
1904 Theodore Roosevelt	45,498,000	13,531,000	29.7
1908 William H. Taft	49,919,000	14,884,000	29.8
1912 Woodrow Wilson	53,830,000	15,037,000	27.9
1916 Woodrow Wilson	57,708,000	18,531,000	32.1
1920 Warren G. Harding	62,988,000	26,748,000	42.5
1924 Calvin Coolidge	66,414,000	29,086,000	43.8
1928 Herbert Hoover	71,185,000	36,812,000	51.7
1932 Franklin D. Roosevelt	75,768,000	39,759,000	52.5
1936 Franklin D. Roosevelt	80,174,000	45,655,000	56.9
1940 Franklin D. Roosevelt	84,728,000	49,900,000	58.9
1944 Franklin D. Roosevelt	85,654,000	47,977,000	56.0
1948 Harry S. Truman	95,573,000	48,794,000	51.1
1952 Dwight D. Eisenhower	99,929,000	61,551,000	61.6
1956 Dwight D. Eisenhower	104,515,000	62,027,000	59.3
1960 John F. Kennedy	109,672,000	68,838,000	63.1
1964 Lyndon B. Johnson	114,090,000	70,645,000	61.9
1968 Richard Nixon	120,285,000	73,212,000	60.9
1972 Richard Nixon	140,777,000	77,719,000	55.2
1976 Jimmy Carter	152,308,000	81,556,000	53.5
1980 Ronald Reagan	164,595,000	86,515,000	52.6
1984 Ronald Reagan	174,468,000	92,653,000	53.1
1988 George Bush	182,779,000	91,595,000	50.1
1992 Bill Clinton	189,044,000	104,423,000	55.2
1996 Bill Clinton	196,507,000	96,278,000	49.0

Sources: Bureau of the Census, *Nonvoting,* Series P-23, No. 102 (Washington, D.C.: U.S. Government Printing Office, 1980); *Presidential Elections, 1789–1996* (Washington, D.C.: Congressional Quarterly, 1997); and Committee for the Study of the American Electorate.

Note: Data prior to 1828 excluded because of the absence of popular elections for presidential electors in many states and the failure to record results in states where popular elections were held. Percentages are based on figures that have been rounded.

Exercises

1. Simulate a meeting of the electoral college in the late eighteenth century. Most electors have been selected by their state legislatures with no popular balloting for presidential aspirants. Each elector has two votes, which must be divided between two candidates. Several candidates have expressed an interest in the presidency and several others in the vice presidency. The top vote-getter will be elected president and the runner-up elected vice president. If no candidate receives a number of votes equal to a majority of electors, the president will be selected by the House of Representatives from the top five candidates. Each state delegation in the House has only one vote. The candidate with the most votes (and a majority) is elected.

Compare this process with the present operation of the electoral college. Is it more or less democratic? Does it produce better or worse presidents?

2. Compare the presidential selection process in the United States in the late eighteenth century with that of the selection of the chief executive in a present-day "new nation" in either Africa or Asia.

3. Most changes in the presidential selection process have been prompted by the dissatisfaction of presidential aspirants with the existing process. For example, the rise of alternative nominating mechanisms to the congressional caucus in the 1820s stemmed from the dissatisfaction of candidates rejected by the caucus. The increasing use of new delegate allocation schemes in the 1970s and 1980s was related to the failure of particular candidates to use the old mechanisms to their advantage.

In the 1996 and 2000 elections many unsuccessful candidates complained about the costs of running and a delegate selection schedule that discriminates against most contenders. Are these complaints loud enough to change the selection process once again?

Discuss by reviewing these complaints, what changes would resolve them and the feasibility of these changes.

4. Technological change has often had a direct impact on the presidential selection process. For example, improved transportation made national nominating conventions possible, and television ultimately changed the way voters evaluate candidates. Identify one major technological change in American history and chart its effect on presidential elections.

5. Significant increases in voter participation in presidential elections have related to particular historical and political events. For example, the increase in voter participation in the 1920 presidential election reflected the votes of newly enfranchised women (see Table 1-4).

Review the trends in voting participation and identify possible political and historical events that might explain these trends. Why were turnouts comparatively high in the 1880s and 1960s? Voter participation in presidential elections has been significantly lower in the past several decades than in the 1950s and 1960s. What might explain this downturn? Would this trend be expected to continue?

6. Voter participation rates in American presidential elections have consistently lagged behind elections in other Western democracies. Compare the election process of another Western democracy with that of the United States. What might explain the differences in voter participation in the two nations?

7. Clear channels of mobility to the presidency exist. Successful presidential aspirants are more likely to reside in particular states and are more likely to have held particular appointed or elected positions (see Table 1-1).

Using data included in this chapter, compare early patterns of mobility to the presidency (1789–1824) with those since 1945. What might account for any differences? What patterns of mobility could be expected in the near future? Why?

Additional Sources

Printed Material and Videos

Fisher, Roger. *Tippecanoe and Trinkets Too.* Urbana: University of Illinois Press, 1988. A delightful analysis of the changing presidential selection process through the material culture of campaigns.

Great American Speeches. Princeton: Films for the Humanities and Sciences, 1997. Thirty-four classic political speeches on video from Theodore Roosevelt's Bull Moose campaign oratory of 1912 to Mario Cuomo's keynote at the 1984 Democratic National Convention. The video is narrated by Jody Powell, former president Jimmy Carter's press secretary, who provides an insightful context for understanding the changing rhetoric and style of the speakers.

Kelly, Kate. *Election Day: An American Holiday, An American History.* New York: Facts on File, 1991. A novel treatment of the changing presidential selection process through a focus on election day.

McGerr, Michael. *The Decline of Popular Politics.* New York: Oxford University Press, 1986. The author charts the relationship of progressive reforms to the decline in public participation in politics. There is much in McGerr's analysis that is relevant to our contemporary political ills.

Overacker, Louise. *The Presidential Primary.* New York: Macmillan, 1926. After all these years, this book is still the classic on the development of the presidential primary and its early use. If your library does not have a copy, it's worth getting one through interlibrary loan.

Presidential Elections, 1789–1996. Washington, D.C.: Congressional Quarterly, 1997. The latest edition of Congressional Quarterly's informed review of the history of American presidential elections. Includes state by state presidential election returns since 1824 and Democratic and Republican primary returns since 1916.

Online Data

American Leaders Speak. This site is part of the Smithsonian Institution's American Memory project. It includes visuals of and voice recordings from leaders during World War I and immediately after. Included is a section on the 1920 presidential election. Users may listen to brief speeches by the candidates, including Franklin D. Roosevelt, the Democratic vice presidential nominee in 1920.

> To access: http://memory.loc.gov/ammem/nfhome.html

America Votes. This site contains presidential campaign memorabilia from Duke University's special collections library. It provides interesting visuals from a number of presidential elections and links to other political and election sites.

> To access: http://odyssey.lib.duke.edu/americavotes/

The Smithsonian Institution and '96 U.S. Presidential Election. A project of the Smithsonian's Internet Archive to collect and store 1996 presidential election materials. Information available includes candidate, party, and parody sites from the 1996 primaries through the general election.

> To access: http://www.archive.org/smithsonian.html

Iowa state auditor Richard Johnson posts the final numbers from the 1999 Iowa straw poll August 14, 1999. Texas governor George W. Bush defeated his Republican rivals in a race in which no delegates were selected but that nonetheless had critical national significance.

(Source: Chris Ocken, Reuters)

2

The Preliminaries

The race for the presidency usually starts long before the national conventions or the primaries or caucuses take place. Potential aspirants may drop hints about running, or an incumbent president may use the powers or resources of office with a reelection bid in mind. Indeed, the preliminaries of a presidential election campaign can begin almost as soon as the returns from the previous election have been tabulated.

Multiyear campaigns have been prompted both by changes in the rules and procedures governing major party nominations and the related increase in the costs of campaigns. Most recently, the appearance of prominent candidates who operate outside the constraints of major party politics or federal campaign finance laws have added additional pressures for longer campaigns. As a result, the incentives for multiyear presidential campaigns have increased significantly, with the 2000 campaign already promising to be one of the longest in recent electoral history.

The Multiyear Campaign

The direct participation of party rank and file in the nomination of major party candidates through primaries has been a characteristic of the presidential selection process since 1912, but only in the past two decades has it become the preferred method of delegate selection. In 1968 about 40 percent of all convention delegates were chosen through primaries. By 1976 this figure had topped 70 percent (see Table 2-1). In this same period, rank-and-file participation in the party caucuses also has been bolstered by changes in party rules that prevent undue manipulation by party officials. As a result, candidates now need the support of primary voters and caucus participants throughout the nation. In the past, major party candidates entered a select number of primaries not because winning delegates would assure them of the nomination but to prove to party leaders that they were potentially electable. Sen. John F. Kennedy, a Roman Catholic, entered and won the 1960 Democratic primary in predominantly Protestant West Virginia, making the point that he would be a viable national candidate if selected by party leaders. Now, rank-and-file participants in primaries and caucuses control the major party nominations.

Because of this change in the presidential selection process, candidates must establish their own base of core supporters early and then rely to a large degree on the mass media to reach the disparate groups of voters who now participate in primaries and caucuses. With the elimination of party leaders from the center of the nomination process, candidates must craft a favorable national image that takes time and careful planning to create.

The role of the media therefore has been a major catalyst to longer campaigns. It takes more time and money for candidates to reach new participants in the presidential selection process through the mass media than it does for them to negotiate with a limited number of party leaders. Furthermore, the mass media tend to focus on candidates they consider front-runners or contenders. Candidates thus must convince the media, long before any votes are cast, that they are electable. Early electoral success in the campaign also becomes a prerequisite to further press coverage. Success, however, is not necessarily based on winning the most or even large numbers of votes in early primaries or caucuses but relates to a more subjective assessment of a candidate's performance by the media.

This role of the media was evident in the 1992 New Hampshire primary. A distant second-place finish by the former front-runner, Arkansas governor Bill Clinton, made him "the comeback kid," a self-characterization the media readily adopted. In the first delegate selection event of 1996, the Louisiana caucuses, Sen. Phil Gramm of Texas lost to journalist Pat Buchanan. Most of the other Republican candidates did not even contest the election. With only 23,000 Republican partisans participating and only twenty-one delegates to the Republican convention at stake (Louisiana would select seven more delegates later in a primary), one national newspaper nonetheless declared Gramm's defeat "a stunning setback." Whatever the exact returns, the story line often becomes the reality. In this case, Gramm suspended his campaign for the presidency eight days after this dismal assessment by the media. In other campaign events in which no delegates are selected, the media also have played an increasingly important role in determining "winners" and "losers." In essence, the new media-based imperatives require candidates to spend years preparing for campaigns that may well end as soon as any delegates to the national conventions are chosen.

Furthermore, the major parties themselves have placed a premium on early starts by candidates. Before reforms in the early 1970s, del-

egates to national nominating conventions were largely selected by party leaders or party conventions over a period of several years. Beginning in 1972 this process was opened significantly to rank-and-file participation and was limited to several months, traditionally beginning with the Iowa caucuses and the New Hampshire primary in February and ending with a round of primaries and state conventions in early June of the election year. Additional "front loading"—selecting more delegates earlier in this shortened time frame—has further accelerated the delegate selection process and compressed it within this brief period (see Figure 2-1). Other states have begun to challenge Iowa and New Hampshire as the traditional starting points for delegate selection, and many states have moved their primary or caucus dates forward in the hope of exerting greater influence in the nominating process. As a result, the delegate selection window for 2000 is virtually a porthole. The majority of delegates selected or bound by primary votes will be chosen in a five-week period in February and March (see Tables 2-2 and 2-3).

Finally, the Federal Election Campaign Act, which is administered by the Federal Election Commission (FEC), has served to extend campaigns by rewarding candidates who start early. To receive matching funds on January 1 of the election year, a candidate must have raised more than $100,000 by collecting more than $5,000 in twenty states in amounts no greater than $250 from any individual contributor. After qualifying for these funds, candidates must conform to specific campaign expenditure limits in every state and to a nationwide expenditure limit. Individual contributions to publicly funded candidates in the primary election process are limited to $1,000, and contributions from political action committees (PACs)—organizations designed to raise and spend money in conjunction with federal elections—are limited to $5,000. Only the first $250 of any individual contribution is matched by public funds. For the pre–general election period in 2000, a maximum of $16.75 million in matching funds is available for each major party candidate. Candidates who take any matching funds are limited to approximately $33 million in campaign expenditures during the 2000 primary election process, plus $6.6 million in fund-raising expenses. Campaigns may also spend unlimited amounts in legal and accounting expenses to comply with the Federal Election Campaign Act. Candidates who accept matching funds can spend no more than $50,000 of their own money. In sum, the act requires presidential aspirants to establish networks of core supporters early in the nomination process to take full advantage of its public financing provisions.

The act also encourages major party candidates to begin their campaigns years in advance by punishing losers and rewarding winners at an early stage in the delegate selection process. Even though only a fraction of delegates are chosen at a single primary, the law eliminates matching funds for any candidate who receives less than 10 percent of the vote in two consecutive primaries. To requalify for public funding, the candidate must receive 20 percent of the vote in a later primary. With the elimination of public funds, private funding for most "losing" candidates becomes problematic.

The media's central role in reaching potential supporters, the compacted schedule for selecting delegates, and the requirements for qualifying for public funding have therefore all been catalysts to earlier and longer campaigns. Candidates now attempt to do as much of their fund raising as possible before the election year. The emergence of candidates operating outside the public financing provisions of the Federal Election Campaign Act (and thus not subject to expenditure limits) and the need for presumptive nominees to continue to raise and spend money in the period between the primaries and caucuses and the convention have also prompted the development of new fund-raising and spending strategies that many consider in violation of campaign finance law.

Third-party and independent candidates operate within a somewhat different strategic context during the campaign preliminaries. Most do not compete in primaries or caucuses, and many do not depend on a convention for nomination. Access to the ballot in the general election is generally secured through a state-by-state petition process. Money and organization are important in funding local activities to support their candidacies, but third-party and independent candidates generally have operated outside the public funding opportunities or constraints of the Federal Election Campaign Act. Most do not qualify as a political party under the law or decide not to participate.

The success of Ross Perot has altered this rule somewhat. In 1992 Perot received the largest vote of any third-party or independent candidate since Theodore Roosevelt in 1912. Perot did not seek either matching funds during the 1992 campaign preliminaries or partial reimbursement after he received the requisite 5 percent of the vote in the general election in November. He did, however, accept partial public funding, amounting to $29 million, for his 1996 campaign. Because of his 8 percent vote in the 1996 election, a Reform Party nominee would again qualify for partial public funding.

Despite these differences, independent and third-party candidates are affected significantly by the campaign preliminaries of the major parties. Their ability to secure a place on the ballot and ultimately to compete in November depends largely on the satisfaction of major party voters with their own nominees. No less important is whether the media consider independent or minor party candidates to be alternatives worthy of coverage.

In sum, the conventional wisdom pertaining to campaign preliminaries, as of 1996, was that candidates must start early to raise funds, develop a base of core supporters, and pursue a positive public image to win a major party nomination. To bring sufficient momentum into early caucuses and primaries, and thereby survive the formative stage of the process, all candidates depend on a positive assessment by the press, and those candidates who desire public financing require certification by the FEC. An early strong showing moves the campaign into the later caucuses and primaries by providing it with national credibility.

This wisdom was largely confirmed by the 1996 campaign. The eventual major party nominees raised the most money and had the strongest organizational bases by the time the delegate selection process began in February. Before formally declaring his candidacy on April 10, 1995, Sen. Robert Dole, the Republican nominee, was able to conduct what was essentially a national campaign, thanks to his leadership PAC, Campaign America, and two foundations, the Better America Foundation and the Dole Foundation. Dole had raised more than $13 million by June 30, 1995, and $24 million by January 1 of election year (see Table 2-4). By the end of March 1996 the Dole campaign had spent $35 million, already approaching the pre–general election limit of $37 million for publicly funded candidates (see Table 2-5). Before the first round of delegate selection, the Dole campaign had amassed endorsements from 130 members of the House and Senate. All the other Republican candidates combined had received only 55 congressional endorsements.

By late January 1996 Dole's campaign had built a formidable national organization staffed by more than 200 paid employees. Only the self-financed campaign of publishing multimillionaire Steve Forbes had the potential to match or surpass Dole in expenditures. Forbes, however, chose to spend heavily in advertising in key early primary and caucus states rather than to build a national campaign organization. Most of Dole's competitors simply did not have the funds or organizational resources to sustain campaigns beyond the opening rounds of an accelerated delegate selection process. By late March, Dole had exhausted his opponents. This strategy also raised the issue of how a presumptive party nominee, who had accepted public funds, could continue to campaign once the expenditure limits had been reached. Efforts by the Republican Party to help ultimately were investigated (although dismissed) by the Federal Election Commission as potentially illegal coordinated efforts between the party and the candidate.

President Clinton's prospects for a second term dimmed considerably with the Republican takeover of Congress in November 1994. Reeling from the worst congressional losses in almost forty years for a party holding the presidency, Clinton was considered vulnerable to challenges from within his own party and to his Republican opponent in the general election. Clinton's head-to-head combat with Republicans in Congress, resulting in two government shutdowns in the winter of 1994–1995, however, improved his prospects. The new Republican congressional majority, headed by Speaker Newt Gingrich of Georgia, soon came to be viewed by the public as uncompromising and unreasonable; the president emerged as a voice of reason. Clinton was also careful not to offend potential presidential contenders within his own party. Although unhappy with Clinton's leadership, potential Democratic rivals quickly realized that their challenges could lose the White House for the Democrats. A GOP win would put Republicans in control of both the executive and legislative branches of government for the first time since 1955. In the end, President Clinton avoided serious challenges for his party's nomination.

As the early presumptive nominee for the Democratic nomination, the president was freed to target the Republicans while they were preoccupied with their own nomination process. By the end of March 1996 Dole's campaign was essentially out of money and rapidly approaching the federally imposed spending limit for publicly funded candidates. President Clinton had $21 million to spend before the Democratic National Convention in August. Not only did the president's early media barrage against the Republicans cripple the eventual Republican nominee, but it raised the question of how much legitimate campaign coordination there could be between the president and Democratic Party committees.

The new Reform Party, energized by an unprecedented 19 percent of the vote for Perot in the 1992 general election, also nominated a presidential candidate in 1996. Although the party's nomination process bore little resemblance to that of the Republicans or the Democrats, it nonetheless reflected a similar dynamic: the candidate with money, national visibility, and resources had a significant advantage. In a preliminary round of voting in preparation for the Reform Party convention, Perot and Richard Lamm, a former governor of Colorado, received enough votes to move to the final round of balloting. Perot, however, had unlimited personal funds, more than $8 million of which he contributed to secure his nomination. Lamm was able to raise only $225,000, of which $30,000 he contributed or loaned (see Table 2-4). Lamm's total was not even enough to canvass Reform Party members before they voted.

The 1996 preliminaries, however, produced surprises, suggesting emerging facets of the nomination process. Despite a narrow victory by front-runner Dole in the Iowa caucuses and a loss to Pat Buchanan in the New Hampshire primary, the Dole campaign held on. None of the other Republican candidates was able to capitalize on what the media generally portrayed as a tepid performance by the front-runner. Indeed, in a drastically compacted window of delegate selection, organization seemed to matter more than media assessments. Among the Republicans, only Dole's presidential campaign had anything that approached a national organization. Even Forbes's self-financed campaign, which could raise unlimited funds (from Forbes himself) could not compete without sufficient staff and organization. In this respect, money in the emerging nomination process is clearly only one component of success. Forbes's challenge, however, reflected the increasing financial pressures that self-financed candidates can place on the nomination process. In essence, Forbes, and any other self-financed candidate, could continue to campaign and spend without public approval or electoral success, while publicly financed candidates were subject to individual contribution and expenditure limits and ultimately would lose both donors and public funds without delegate selection victories.

New Campaign Preliminaries

To navigate the waters successfully before declaring their candidacy, potential candidates have developed sophisticated and prolonged precampaign strategies. Their goal is to gain positive national visibility and develop local networks of volunteers and financial supporters before they are subject to the contribution and expenditure limits of the Federal Election Campaign Act. This flexibility is increasingly important because of the likelihood that the period before the general election campaign will now involve self-financed candidates who personally may contribute unlimited amounts of money to their own campaign and will not be subject to expenditure limits. The precampaign activities of Lamar Alexander, Bill Bradley, and Steve Forbes perhaps best reflect the variety and ingenuity related to these new imperatives.

Former Tennessee governor and secretary of education Lamar Alexander withdrew from the race for the 1996 Republican nomination on March 6 after he failed to win any of the early caucuses or primaries. As Alexander conceded defeat, he immediately geared up a multifaceted, sophisticated effort to build support and make friends for another presidential bid in 2000. From July to November 1996 Alexander's federal PAC, Campaign for a New American Century, made thirty-one contributions, totaling more than $70,000, to Republican candidates for the Senate and House. His federal PAC raised more than $1.5 million in 1997 and $2.6 million in 1998. In both years a significant portion of these receipts ($700,000 in 1997 and $1.9 million in 1998) were transferred from state PACs controlled by Alexander to be spent on joint state-federal activities whose overall goal was to promote Alexander. During this period, Campaign for a New American Century made eighteen contributions, totaling $30,000, to Republican House and Senate candidates. The largest contributions clearly reflected election 2000 considerations, almost always going to Republican candidates in the critical early delegate selection states, Iowa and New Hampshire. Alexander's federal PAC also maintained "soft money" (nonfederal) accounts, which allowed it to give money to state parties or to nonfederal accounts of the national parties. In 1998 it made contributions to two nonfederal accounts of the Republican National Committee.

Alexander's use of state PACs transformed his ability to raise and spend money in the gray areas or outside the limits of federal campaign finance law. Alexander established state PACs in Delaware, New Hampshire, Oklahoma, South Carolina, Tennessee, and Virginia. These PACs raised money nationwide, often under lax state limits, and either transferred money to a federal PAC for joint activities or made contributions directly to state candidates or state parties. In 1998 Alexander's state PACs supported Republican candidates or Republican state parties in eighteen states, with most contributions directed to candidates in Alexander's home state of Tennessee or to candidates in Iowa and New Hampshire. One of Alexander's Virginia PACs, We the Parents, raised $1.8 million in its first months of operation in 1999; this figure included twelve contributions of $30,000–$100,000, which would have been prohibited as "hard money" contributions to a federal PAC under federal campaign law. By the time Alexander declared his candidacy on March 9, 1999, he had already spent years making friends and soliciting support throughout the nation, all through federal and state PACs. None of this activity was considered part of a presidential campaign or subject to expenditure limits under federal campaign finance law.

Alexander's activity involved the careful pursuit of a national donor network to support another presidential campaign, whereas former New Jersey Democratic senator Bill Bradley used a very different strategy. Bradley's biggest asset is his name recognition, derived from his star status as a professional basketball player in the 1960s and 1970s, not his fund-raising abilities. Bradley's precampaign goal therefore was to keep his name before the American people and, in the process, to solidify his image as a reformer.

After retiring from the Senate in 1997, Bradley continued to build his national image as chairman of the National Civic League, as cochair of Project Independence, a joint venture with Common Cause and Public Citizen to reform campaign finance laws, and as cochair of the Advertising Council's efforts to create advertising that would benefit children. These efforts kept Bradley in front of the American public and also provided him with opportunities to interact with potential campaign donors. Bradley established his own Web site and wrote a column, "Bill Bradley Listening" for ThirdAge.com in which he urged readers to "share your story with Bill Bradley." In a more traditional vein, he reported on American life for CBS's weekend evening news and hosted a four-part series, called *Uncommon Americans*, on A&E Television Networks. Friends of Bradley also started an online Bill Bradley Network, where supporters could participate in "Bradley forums." According to this site, "Here you can discuss campaign strategies with other Bradley supporters from all over the nation."

Although Bradley's efforts were oriented toward gaining publicity, they did not ignore the new reality of all precampaign periods— the search for ways to raise and spend substantial sums before a making a formal declaration of candidacy. Bradley transformed his Senate Campaign Committee into a leadership PAC, Time Future, which raised almost $400,000 in 1998 and made a total of $104,000 in contributions to fifty Democratic candidates for the House and ten for the Senate in 1997–1998. Time Future in 1998 also made soft money donations to nonfederal accounts of the Democratic Senatorial Campaign Committee. In New Hampshire, Bradley established a state PAC that raised money out of state and contributed to the campaign of the Democratic gubernatorial candidate. Bradley also remains associated with another federal PAC, Participation 2000, which raised and spent approximately $350,000 in the 1997–1998 election cycle. Participation 2000 does not donate directly to candidates. Instead, it provides recent college graduates with training, including a one-week summer session with Bradley, and then assigns them to work in Democratic campaigns. In the process, Bradley has effectively developed a national network of loyal supporters.

If Bradley's financial operations appear small or unsophisticated compared with those of Alexander, some of this difference was by design. Bradley's major appeal and potential positioning in the race for the Democratic nomination against Vice President Al Gore was as the "clean" candidate in the dirty world of campaign finance. Despite Bradley's rhetoric of changing the rules of the political money game, however, he is a prodigious fund-raiser in the traditional mode. As he moved into the official stage of his campaign, he outraised every other presidential candidate except Gore and Texas governor George W. Bush Jr. (see Table 2-6). And he surpassed Bush and Gore in the number of individual contributions at the maximum allowed under the law—$1,000.

Steve Forbes's precampaign efforts are especially important because they have, more than the activities of any other early aspirant, redefined what candidates must do before they formally declare their candidacy. Forbes is able to tap a vast personal fortune. This means that, because most of his campaign contributions are his own, he avoids the expenditure limits tied to public funding and does not have to wrestle with federal PAC or personal contribution limits. In essence, Forbes can run unfettered by financial considerations. This advantage is best reflected by the fact that in January 1999 the 1996 Forbes campaign continued to carry a $37 million debt that did not have to be repaid because virtually all of it was owed to the candidate himself.

During the 2000 precampaign period, Forbes began to build on the lessons of his failed 1996 campaign for the Republican nomination, in which a top-down strategy fueled by money alone was not enough to win. Forbes's new bottom-up strategy has involved his federal PAC, Americans for Hope, Growth, and Opportunity, and state PACs by the same name in Iowa and New Hampshire. Through these vehicles he has contributed to federal and state candidates. To increase his visibility in the 1997–1998 election cycle, Forbes's federal PAC raised more than $95,000 and contributed to five Republican House and Senate candidates, two of whom were from Iowa. His Iowa PAC gave $5,000 to the reelection campaign of the speaker of the Iowa House, while his New Hampshire PAC supported candidates for the state's executive council.

Part of Forbes's new strategy has been to make friends and recruit potential supporters through his public charity, also named Americans for Hope, Growth, and Opportunity. Gifts from this charity to conservative organizations have given him new credibility and reach beyond economic conservatives. Similarly, he has cemented relationships with conservative grassroots organizations and recruited their members into his campaign. This strategy was evident in his March 16, 1999, formal declaration of candidacy when he identified himself as an economic and social conservative who would run a "citizen's campaign."

Precampaign activities therefore suggest both the resources of potential candidates and their probable strategies for nomination once they become declared candidates. Potential candidates may have a combination of resources, but rarely do they have all the vital ingredients for success: name recognition, abundant financial resources, committed followers, extensive party connections, and a national organization. Different resources inevitably mean different strategies. In the current compacted schedule of selecting delegates, underfunded campaigns can at most hope to damage a front-runner in an early primary or caucus. Campaigns with followers but not necessarily money are especially suited to waging battle in small states that select delegates early but not in large primary states where expensive advertising is a requirement. Campaigns with unlimited money (generally those that are self-financed or not publicly funded) may be able to afford extensive advertising in major media markets, but they often lack the followers and organization needed to recruit volunteers and get out the vote.

Resources and strategies also relate to the ideological positioning of the candidate. Campaigns with followers or with grassroots, such as those of Pat Buchanan or conservative activist Gary Bauer, tend to be anchored in distinct ideological segments of the party or identified with very specific issues. Although ideology may be helpful in primaries and caucuses in relatively homogeneous and small states, it becomes a detriment to attracting a wider spectrum of voters in larger, more heterogeneous states. On the other hand, well-funded campaigns with high-name-recognition candidates, such as that of Governor Bush, face the opposite problem. With broad positive personal appeal, these candidates tend to avoid identifying with strident policy stances or single issues. In this regard, their support may be wide but shallow. As a result, many potential voters in primaries or caucuses may not know where these candidates stand on critical issues. For example, in late May 1999 voters continued to rate Bush slightly more in tune with their own views than Elizabeth Dole, one of his chief competitors. This belief was in spite of Dole's high-visibility efforts to stake out more moderate positions on gun control and abortion, while Bush remained largely silent on these issues.

Because the media regard defining candidates as a critical part of their job, front-running candidates with broad-based support are especially at risk. Through the first half of 1999, Bush's response was a "front porch campaign," a Texas-based strategy designed to buffer the candidate from the national press. Although this technique was successful in maintaining high favorability ratings for Bush, his general inaccessibility frustrated the media, often angering them. In the midst of the Balkan crisis, the *Wall Street Journal,* for example, attacked Bush's stance as "so vague and tepid as to be almost Clintonian."

To prepare for a brutally brief schedule of delegate selection for the nominating conventions, potential candidates and formally declared candidates have participated in and initiated an increasing number of campaign preliminaries. The days when a prospective candidate could start campaigning in the spring of an election year, as Gen. Dwight D. Eisenhower did when he returned to the United States from Europe in April 1952, seem far removed from the realities of the present nomination process.

These new and voluminous campaign preliminaries include efforts to introduce the candidate to the general public as well as more directed attempts to recruit the party faithful. These latter endeavors often involve events sponsored by the party or interest groups in which candidates have the opportunity to appear or compete. Although none of these is directly related to the selection of delegates to the nominating conventions, each nevertheless has a significant effect on the success of major party candidates in securing the nomination and on the viability of minor party or independent candidates.

Democrats and Republicans have employed both of these strategies in the 2000 preliminaries. Candidates with easy and regular access to the media hone their images with a run for the White House in mind. Vice President Gore, the clear front-runner for the Democratic nomination, has used his elected position to expand his portfolio of issues. High-visibility statements on new domestic issues and the Balkan crisis convey the image of a seasoned leader ready to step comfortably into the presidency. Other candidates, without the guaranteed media access provided a high elected official, must contrive events for the media that, if covered, will begin to convey the candidate's message. The Balkan war, for example, provided Elizabeth Dole, former head of the American Red Cross, the opportunity to visit refugee camps in Macedonia and to make well publicized statements on American foreign policy—an opportunity she might not otherwise have had. In late June 1999 the release of Governor Bush's prodigious second-quarter fund-raising receipts (see Table 2-6), along with the announcement that his campaign would operate outside the public funding provisions of the Federal Election Campaign Act, gave Sen. John McCain, R-Ariz., an opportunity to highlight his own credentials as a campaign finance reformer.

An event that usually draws significant media coverage is the candidate's formal declaration of running for office. Both the venue and the speech are carefully constructed to convey to the public what may be the candidate's first and lasting impression. At the March 10, 1999, announcement of her campaign exploratory committee, Elizabeth Dole was flanked by a teacher, a farmer, and a twelve-year-old girl who hoped someday to be president. Two high school bands helped kick off the announcement, while photos of Dole with former president Ronald Reagan, various military figures, and television host Jay Leno provided the backdrop at the convention center in Des Moines, Iowa. For election 2000, Lamar Alexander had rethought his failed 1996 strategy. Gone was the flannel shirt donned by the citizen-candidate who was about to walk the early campaign trail to meet the voters. This second time around Alexander announced his candidacy at the old state courthouse in Nashville, Tennessee. Surrounded by American flags, he wore business attire and was flanked by the governors of Arkansas and Tennessee. The announcements of Forbes and McCain provided voters with clear campaign messages. On March 16, 1999, Forbes made his declaration online, stressing that this was the beginning of a "new information age campaign." McCain, a former prisoner of war in Vietnam and an advocate of U.S. ground troops in Yugoslavia, postponed his announcement and a related tour because of the crisis in the Balkans. He finally declared on April 14, 1999, in a news release,

saying, "Now is not the time for the celebratory tour I had planned."

Candidates also attempt to attract media attention and generate images of growing voter support through endorsements by other politicians or heads of influential organizations. For example, Gore took full advantage of the endorsement of his erstwhile opponent, House minority leader Richard Gephardt. This endorsement was made in Manchester, New Hampshire, the first stop on Gore's first official trip of his campaign. At a giant photo opportunity, Gephardt, with the appropriate backdrop of American flags, told a rally of 400 Gore supporters, "I'm here today because I want to make my fight putting Al Gore in the presidency." When Gore was plagued in the spring of 1999 by a series of rhetorical missteps, he received an endorsement from forty-four of the forty-seven Democrats in the California state assembly. As one assembly woman put it, "We believe [Gore] needs a boost."

Candidates also use public opinion polls to bolster positive perception or to raise questions about their opponents' viability. This often involves what one national pollster labels "happy polling," in which the candidate's pollsters cast their net so widely and loosely that at least some good news is ensured. Polling by candidates is supplemented by extensive public opinion research by the television networks and news magazines. Releases of these polls become campaign events that mold public perception. Most of these early polls, however, reflect little more than name recognition. For example, in April 1999 a Reuters poll found Governor Bush—with 47 percent of the preferences—leading all other Republican candidates among likely Republican voters. However, when the names of the candidates were removed from the question and replaced with brief biographies, Bush's support fell to 24 percent.

The second category of increasingly important campaign preliminaries includes events sponsored by the local Democratic or Republican Parties or by nonparty groups that wish to be wooed by candidates. In some cases, votes or "straw polls" are taken among the audience. These events serve as forums for candidates to reveal their platforms and to provide them with necessary visibility. These are especially important for candidates who are not front-runners or who do not hold an elected office that can serve as a platform to gain publicity.

As early as August 1997 Republican presidential hopefuls flocked to the Midwestern Republican Leadership Conference, which had been billed as the first preview of the 2000 presidential race. Speakers included Governor Bush, House Speaker Newt Gingrich, former vice presidential nominee Jack Kemp, former vice president Dan Quayle, and Sen. Fred Thompson of Tennessee. At the Southern Republican Leadership Conference in March 1998, more than 1,100 delegates cast straw ballots for both president and vice president. At the annual meetings of the Conservative Political Action Conference in January 1998 and January 1999, participants cast their ballots for president. Forbes won in 1998; conservative activist Gary Bauer won in 1999. And the Republican Parties in Iowa and New Hampshire sponsored meetings in 1998 and 1999 at which most Republican contenders spoke. Candidate Elizabeth Dole used the May 1999 New Hampshire meeting to advocate stricter gun controls and thereby position herself before the national press as the only moderate in the Republican field.

Although the race for the 2000 nomination on the Democratic side narrowed early to two candidates, party or interest group forums nonetheless remained vital. Both the Bradley and the Gore campaigns saw the April 1999 midterm convention of the New Hampshire Democratic Party as a prime opportunity to perfect their message before an attentive national media. Bradley made a thinly veiled attack on President Clinton's character, while Tipper Gore (representing her husband) focused on a host of unresolved domestic issues. Their presentations suggested the early outline of the race for the Democratic nomination. During the convention charges were also made that the Bradley campaign had bused in supporters to ensure a positive response to the former senator.

Finally, candidates today are willing to debate each other to gain positive media coverage. Televised debates offer candidates the opportunity to reach millions of voters. They provide candidates with free media exposure and a chance to outshine opponents and test new themes and styles. The cost, however, may be a losing performance by one of the candidates or a particularly dramatic moment that starkly defines them, for better or worse, before a national public. In 1980 Republican front-runners George Bush and Ronald Reagan could not agree on what other Republican candidates should be included in a debate in Nashua, New Hampshire. Reagan, who had already lost the Iowa caucuses and therefore needed a campaign boost, agreed to pay all the costs associated with the debate. Bush, however, insisted that he would debate only Reagan. With several Republican candidates waiting in the wings and the Republican front-runners already on stage, Reagan took charge. In a decisive moment, he proclaimed that all the candidates would debate because "I am paying for this microphone." In a few seconds before a local New Hampshire audience and a national television audience, Reagan established himself as a take-charge leader, while Bush appeared ineffectual at best. Although it is unclear whether Reagan's remark was planned or spontaneous, Spencer Tracy has a comparable line in *State of the Union,* a 1948 film directed by Frank Capra about a millionaire aircraft manufacturer who is seeking the Republican presidential nomination.

Virtually all the new campaign preliminaries reflect the growing importance of the media. Candidates desperately need media exposure. But in providing this exposure, the media ultimately comment and interpret. As one observer facetiously put it, "What the media giveth, it can taketh away." The 1996 preliminaries may have altered conventional notions as to where and when the media are most influential, but they also reaffirmed the role the media now perform in the presidential nominating process and prompted candidates to search for ways to avoid constant media scrutiny.

The 2000 preliminaries promise more of the same. In the spring of 1999 the media pounced on several gaffes by Vice President Gore. First emphasizing his rural background, despite the fact that he grew up in Washington, D.C., and then claiming he had played a seminal role in the creation of the Internet, despite the fact that he was barely in law school when Congress first funded it, Gore was forced to explain his assertions. Even more damaging, however, was the rapid transformation of these stories into camp humor. Largely undefined by the public, Gore suddenly was at risk of emerging as a Dan Quayle—a candidate who may never shed the media-imposed image of a lightweight. In this regard, there is no doubt that the media will continue to be an important actor, but exactly in what circumstances and through what means candidates will be able to avoid media control of the campaign will become clear only as the overall outline of a quickly changing presidential selection process emerges.

2000 Delegate Selection Rules

Just as the road to the convention has become long and tortuous, so have the rules for the selection of delegates to major party conventions become increasingly complex. New rules for selecting delegates that were adopted by the Democratic National Committee in 1990 and 1994 furthered this trend by balancing previous reforms that emphasized rank-and-file control of the process with a new emphasis on increased participation by elected and appointed Democratic Party officials. The basic Democratic rules governing delegate selection for 2000 are the following:

• Primaries and caucuses must be held between the first Tuesday in March and the second Tuesday in June of 2000, with some exceptions (see Table 2-2).

• Delegates are not formally bound to candidates but "in all good conscience should reflect the sentiments of those who elected them."

• Candidates must receive 15 percent of the statewide primary or caucus votes to be allocated statewide delegates.

• In both primary and caucus states, candidates must receive 15 percent of the vote in a particular district to be allocated district delegates.

• Seventy-five percent of the base allocation of delegates to each state (the total state delegation minus pledged or unpledged party officials) must be elected at the congressional district level.

• Each state delegation will be supplemented by an additional 15 percent of delegate slots. These additional slots will be apportioned to big-city mayors, state-wide elected officials, state legislators, and other state, county, and local elected officials who will be pledged delegates. Each state delegation will also be supplemented by delegate slots filled by present or former elected national leaders and party leaders. These delegates are officially unpledged.

• All delegations to the convention must be equally divided between men and women.

For the Democrats the changes from 1996 to 2000 in the rules governing delegate selection are relatively minor. Loopholes and bonus allocation schemes, which reward winning candidates with additional delegates, again are prohibited. The continuing emphasis on the equal division of convention delegations between men and women is upheld with the specification that district-level delegates, who are selected before at-large delegates, must conform to this rule. All state delegations again are expanded by 15 percent to ensure inclusion of party officials, and approximately 18 percent of all convention slots again are allocated to present and former elected and appointed officials who will attend as formally unpledged delegates (or, as the media have labeled them, "superdelegates"). Automatically included as unpledged delegates are the president and vice president (if they are

Democrats), former Democratic presidents and vice presidents, former Democratic leaders of the U.S. Senate and former Speakers and minority leaders of the House, former chairs of the Democratic National Committee, and current Democratic governors and members of Congress. This provision precludes the necessity in 2000 for either House or Senate Democrats to meet to select their delegates, as was the case before 1996.

Although the Republicans' rules for selecting and allocating delegates to their national convention have also changed, these rules reflect a much more consistent approach on the part of the national Republican Party than do those of their Democratic counterparts. The national Republican Party historically has been loath to mandate delegate selection procedures, but concern about the excessive front loading of delegate selection prompted the GOP to establish a window for primaries and caucuses for the 2000 campaign season. This official period of delegate selection begins with the first Monday in February and ends with the third Tuesday in June of election year. More in tune with their historical laissez-faire approach to state delegate selection procedures, Republicans also established a voluntary scheme whereby states would be rewarded with additional delegates for primaries and caucuses that came later in the year. Despite these changes for 2000, state Republican Parties retain considerably more freedom than do their Democratic equivalents in establishing rules governing their representation at the national nominating convention. As a result, state Republican Parties essentially choose the form of election used to select delegates, the formulas that allocate delegates on the basis of popular votes, and the rules that bind elected delegates according to the preferences of Republican voters in primaries or caucuses.

As a result of these differences, Republican and Democratic delegate selection in 2000 will proceed at a slightly different pace, with the Republicans beginning slightly before the Democrats. Republicans will also permit a greater variety of mechanisms for allocating delegates based on primary or caucus results, including some allocation schemes that Democrats have outlawed.

In sum, the delegate selection process for 2000 will follow a myriad of distinct party rules. For example, on February 8, 2000, both New Hampshire Republicans and Democrats are scheduled to hold their parties' first primaries of the delegate selection season. The similarity, however, ends there. On the Republican side, all seventeen delegates will be allotted proportionally, based on the statewide vote. To receive delegates, a candidate's vote must total at least 10 percent statewide. Delegates are pledged to their original presidential preference unless that candidate withdraws.

On the Democratic side, fourteen delegates will be elected on the basis of congressional districts, while five will be elected statewide. District delegates will be allotted proportionally on the basis of the district vote, while statewide delegates will be apportioned on the basis of the statewide vote. In each case, a candidate must receive at least 15 percent of the vote to be allotted delegates. District delegates will select three other delegates, who are pledged to candidates in proportion to the statewide primary vote. These delegate positions are reserved for state and local elected officials, such as statewide officers, mayors, or state legislative leaders. Finally, seven other unpledged delegates will be selected as part of the New Hampshire delegation to the Democratic National Convention; these will include members of the Democratic National Committee who reside in New Hampshire, the governor (who is a Democrat), and one additional delegate. Except for the officially unpledged delegates, all delegates are required "in all good conscience" to reflect the sentiments of the voters who elected them.

For minor parties that have qualified as recognized political parties in New Hampshire, February 8, 2000, will also be primary day. For independent candidates, access to the general election ballot involves a petition process that requires the submission of the signatures of 3,000 legal voters by August 7.

The road to nomination is long and complex. Independent and minor party candidates must deal with fifty separate sets of rules to qualify for the general election ballot in the fifty states. Major party candidates are subject to a complex array of rules governing the allocation of delegates and to the evaluation of more than fifty electorates throughout the primary and caucus process. In the past, individual steps in the nominating process were exaggerated, with the Iowa caucuses and the New Hampshire primary having a disproportionate effect on the pre–general election stage. With both parties approaching what is effectively a national primary in 2000, however, it is unclear what role the individual primaries or caucuses may play.

As the chair of the Republican National Committee put it, the 2000 primaries and caucuses may well operate "like a string of firecrackers," providing little opportunity for media winnowing or public learning in between lightning explosions of primary and caucus results.

The race for the presidency reaches truly national proportions only in the late summer of election year. At that time the two national parties gather in their separate conventions to nominate their candidates for the presidency, and minor party or independent candidates are completing the state-by-state process of gaining access to the general election ballot. The candidates then present themselves to a national electorate at a single election in November. The winner has the unique responsibility of representing all Americans.

Table 2-1 The Growth of Presidential Primaries, 1968–1996

	Republican Party			Democratic Party			
Year	Number of primaries	Votes cast	Delegates selected through primaries (in percent)	Number of primaries	Votes cast	Delegates selected through primaries (in percent)	Total delegates selected through primaries (in percent)
1968	15	7,535,069	40.2	15	4,473,551	38.1	39.1
1972	21	15,993,965	65.3	20	6,188,281	56.8	61.0
1976	27	16,052,652	76.0	26	10,374,125	71.0	73.5
1980	35	18,747,825	71.8	35	12,690,451	76.0	73.7
1984	30	18,009,217	52.4	25	6,575,651	71.0	59.6
1988	37	22,961,936	66.6	37	12,165,115	76.9	70.2
1992	40	20,239,385	66.9	39	12,696,547	83.9	72.7
1996	36	10,963,044	65.3	43	15,301,688	84.6	69.2

Source: Selecting the President from 1789 to 1996 (Washington, D.C.: Congressional Quarterly, 1997).

FIGURE 2-1   The Rise of Front Loading in Delegate Selection, 1968–2000

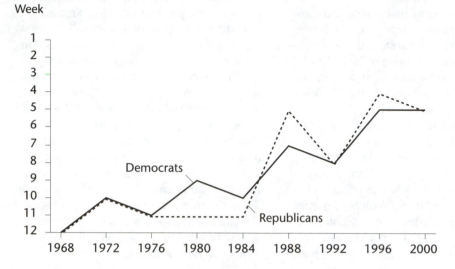

Note: The data show the number of weeks from the first primary until a majority of primary delegates are selected. Calculations include only delegates selected or bound by primary votes. For example, in 2000 this would include pledged Democratic delegates who are allocated on the basis of a primary vote. Democratic and Republican calculations for 2000 are based on the preliminary delegate selection schedule as of July 1999.

Table 2-2 2000 Democratic Delegate Selection Calendar: Primaries and Caucuses

Date	State	Apportionment method	Total delegate votes [a]
February 7	Iowa	Caucus	56
February 8	New Hampshire	Primary	29
February 12	Delaware[b]	Primary	22
	Michigan[b]	Primary	156
February 19	South Carolina[b]	Primary	52
February 29	Washington[b]	Primary	94
March 7	American Samoa	Caucus	6
	California	Primary	434
	Connecticut	Primary	67
	Georgia	Primary	92
	Hawaii	Caucus	33
	Maine	Primary	32
	Maryland	Primary	91
	Massachusetts	Primary	118
	Missouri	Primary	92
	New York	Primary	292
	North Dakota	Caucus	22
	Ohio	Primary	170
	Rhode Island	Primary	32
	Vermont	Primary	22

Table 2-2 *Continued*

Date	State	Apportionment method	Total delegate votes [a]
March 10	Colorado	Primary	61
	Utah	Primary	29
	Wyoming	Primary	18
March 11	Arizona	Primary	56
	Minnesota	Caucus	90
March 11–13	Democrats Abroad	Caucus	9
March 12	Nevada	Caucus	30
	Puerto Rico	Primary	59
March 14	Florida	Primary	185
	Louisiana	Primary	74
	Mississippi	Primary	46
	Oklahoma	Primary	51
	Oregon	Primary	58
	Tennessee	Primary	81
	Texas	Primary and caucus	231
March 21	Illinois	Primary	190
March 25	Alaska	Caucus	19
April 1	Virgin Islands	Caucus	6
April 4	Kansas	Primary	42
	Wisconsin	Primary	92
April 15-17	Virginia	Caucus	99
April 25	Pennsylvania	Primary	191
May 2	District of Columbia	Primary	32
	Indiana	Primary	89
	North Carolina	Primary	103
May 6	Guam	Caucus	6
May 9	Nebraska	Primary	32
	West Virginia	Primary	43
May 23	Arkansas	Primary	48
	Idaho	Primary	23
	Kentucky	Primary	58
June 6	Alabama	Primary	65
	Montana	Primary	24
	New Jersey	Primary	124
	New Mexico	Primary	35
	South Dakota	Primary	22

Source: Democratic National Committee.

Note: Dates listed are for primaries or first-round caucuses. Nonbinding or "beauty contest" primaries are excluded. In some cases, the actual selection of individuals to be delegates may occur later or through a separate process on a different schedule. Primary and caucus dates and method of selection are those in effect on July 1, 1999.

[a] "Total delegate votes" include both delegates apportioned through the primary or caucus process and unpledged delegates or "superdelegates."

[b] Proposed dates for Delaware, Michigan, South Carolina, and Washington are in violation of Democratic National Committee rules and therefore are especially subject to change.

Table 2-3 2000 Republican Delegate Selection Calendar: Primaries and Caucuses

Date	State	Apportionment method	Total delegate votes[a]
January 24	Alaska	Caucus	44
	Louisiana	Caucus	28
February 7	Iowa	Caucus	25
February 8	New Hampshire	Primary	17
February 12	Delaware	Primary	12
February 19	South Carolina	Primary	37
February 22	Arizona	Primary	30
	Michigan	Primary	58
February 26	American Samoa	Caucus	4
	Guam	Caucus	4
	Virgin Islands	Caucus	4
February 27	Puerto Rico	Primary	14
February 29	North Dakota	Caucus	19
	Virginia	Primary	55
March 7	California	Primary	162
	Connecticut	Primary	25
	Georgia	Primary	54
	Maine	Primary	14
	Maryland	Primary	31
	Massachusetts	Primary	37
	Missouri	Primary	35
	New York	Primary	101
	Ohio	Primary	69
	Rhode Island	Primary	14
	Vermont	Primary	12
	Washington	Caucus	37
March 10	Colorado	Primary	40
	Utah	Primary	29
	Wyoming	Caucus	22
March 14	Florida	Primary	80
	Mississippi	Primary	33
	Oklahoma	Primary	38
	Oregon	Primary	24
	Tennessee	Primary	37
	Texas	Primary	124
March 21	Illinois	Primary	74
April 4	Kansas	Primary	35
	Wisconsin	Primary	37
April 25	Minnesota	Caucus	34
	Pennsylvania	Primary	80
May 2	District of Columbia	Primary	15
	Indiana	Primary	55
	North Carolina	Primary	62
May 9	Nebraska	Primary	30
	West Virginia	Primary	18
May 15	Kentucky[b]	Caucus	30
May 19	Hawaii	Caucus	14
May 23	Arkansas	Primary	24
	Idaho	Primary	28
	Kentucky[b]	Primary	30

Table 2-3 *Continued*

Date	State	Apportionment method	Total delegate votes[a]
June 6	Alabama	Primary	44
	Montana	Primary	23
	New Jersey	Primary	54
	New Mexico	Primary	21
	South Dakota	Primary	22

Source: Republican National Committee.

Note: Dates listed are for primaries or first-round caucuses. Nonbinding or "beauty contest" primaries are excluded. In some cases, the actual selection of individuals to be delegates may occur later or through a separate process on a different schedule. Primary and caucus dates and method of selection are those in effect on July 1, 1999.

[a] "Total delegate votes" include both delegates apportioned through the primary or caucus process and others who may be appointed by state party leadership regardless of primary or caucus results. Total delegates are preliminary allocations as of July 21, 1999.

[b] Kentucky is listed twice because the state Republican Party allocates delegates both on the basis of caucuses and a primary held on different dates.

Table 2-4 1996 Candidates' Pre–General Election Receipts

Candidate	Source of receipt				
	Federal matching funds	Individuals	Party and committees	Candidate	Other
Democrats					
Clinton	$13,412,194	$28,314,898	$42,441	—	$517,095
LaRouche	624,691	3,200,051	1,020	—	150
Republicans					
Alexander	4,573,442	12,635,365	286,766	9,583	128,170
Buchanan	10,540,992	15,514,355	18,280	—	437,944
Dole	13,545,767	29,831,933	1,226,172	—	65,555
Dornan	—	298,271	1,000	44,000	4,374
Forbes	—	4,203,692	2,000	37,394,000	31,265
Gramm	7,356,218	15,879,881	402,866	—	376,832
Keyes	1,263,408	3,447,623	1,501	7,500	11,393
Lugar	2,657,242	4,804,212	135,265	—	102,033
Specter	1,010,455	2,280,106	158,791	—	19,148
Taylor	—	37,854	—	6,475,096	3,900
Wilson	1,724,254	5,568,808	253,949	—	108,723
Other					
Browne (LI)	—	1,450,757	2,794	34,271	—
Hagelin (NL)	504,826	723,218	100	15,550	4
Lamm (RF)	—	195,788	—	30,000	—
Perot (RF)	—	104,465	—	8,852,575	—

Source: Federal Election Commission.

Note: Receipts reported to the FEC as of December 31, 1996.

LI = Libertarian; NL = Natural Law; RF = Reform

Table 2-5 1996 Candidates' Pre–General Election Expenditures

	Type of expenditure		
Candidate	Operating expenditures plus fund raising	Exempt legal and accounting expenses	Other
Democrats			
Clinton	$36,353,333	$4,067,790	$29,601
LaRouche	3,706,091	3,787	172,145
Republicans			
Alexander	14,193,426	2,245,635	—
Buchanan	25,510,552	—	—
Dole	37,634,960	4,466,236	566,271
Dornan	343,683	1,081	—
Forbes	41,615,674	—	14,250
Gramm	25,145,610	2,957,536	55,785
Keyes	4,571,852	—	7,000
Lugar	7,571,896	100,293	—
Specter	3,404,681	—	—
Taylor	6,497,181	—	3,410
Wilson	6,256,840	998,286	21,506
Other			
Browne (LI)	1,451,477	—	—
Hagelin (NL)	1,240,035	—	—
Lamm (RF)	197,609	—	—
Perot (RF)	8,469,165	—	—

Source: Federal Election Commission.
Note: Expenditures reported to the FEC as of December 31,1996.
LI = Libertarian; RF = Reform; NL = Natural Law

Table 2-6 Financial Activity of 1999–2000 Presidential Campaigns

Candidate	Receipts	Expenditures	Cash on hand
Democrats			
Bradley	$11,748,225	$4,292,175	$7,496,610
Gore	19,559,571	8,211,047	12,428,594
LaRouche	694,610	694,159	5,550
Republicans			
Alexander	2,528,218	2,437,467	90,750
Bauer	3,441,632	3,097,206	344,425
Buchanan	2,448,080	1,900,385	547,695
Bush	37,289,782	7,209,890	30,079,891
Dole	3,513,942	1,699,091	1,816,355
Forbes	9,513,946	8,307,203	1,205,140
Hatch[a]	—	—	—
Kasich	3,131,394	1,195,318	1,936,076
Keyes	1,914,847	1,742,349	172,497
McCain	6,314,332	3,670,263	2,664,069
Quayle	3,502,247	3,369,380	128,750

Table 2-6 *Continued*

Candidate	Receipts	Expenditures	Cash on hand
Other			
Smith[b]	1,589,543	1,197,760	391,783

Source: Federal Election Commission.

Note: Activity reported to the FEC through June 30, 1999.

[a] Hatch is not required to file financial reports with the Federal Election Commission until October 15, 1999.

[b] Smith left the Republican Party on July 13, 1999, to pursue the presidential nomination as an independent.

Exercises

1. You are a citizen in the state of New Columbia, which sends twenty delegates to the national convention. Today the presidential primary election takes place. Assuming that your classmates are fellow citizens of New Columbia, conduct a primary with the following rule:

• The presidential candidate who receives the most votes receives all twenty delegates.

Hold the election a second time, with each student voting for the same candidate as in the first election. For the second election, however, use the following rules:

• The class is divided into four equal groups.

• The presidential candidate who receives the most votes in each group receives five delegates.

Hold the election a third time, with students again voting for the same candidate. For this election, use the following rules:

• The class is divided into four equal groups.

• In each group, all candidates who receive 15 percent or more of the vote are allotted one to four delegates based on their share of the vote. Candidates receiving less than 15 percent of the vote win no delegates.

Compare the results of each election in terms of delegate allocation. Which seems the fairest? Which is the most "representative" of the electorate?

2. In 2000 the majority of delegates to the major party nominating conventions will be chosen in the shortest time period ever. Indeed, this delegate selection schedule approximates a national primary. Analyze the characteristics of the 2000 pre–general election period in terms of the effects of the new schedule. Was media coverage of the primaries and caucuses different? Did different kinds of candidates win? Were candidates' strategies different? Did money matter more? Are any of the differences you have identified good or bad for the presidential selection process? Explain.

3. Select a state and analyze the Democratic or Republican caucus or primary results. What might explain those results?

4. Select one Republican or Democratic candidate and analyze his or her strategy before the selection of delegates for the 2000 national convention. How did this candidate communicate first with core supporters and later with the broader public? What precampaign strategies did the candidate use? What setting did the candidate use for his or her declaration of candidacy? Compare your candidate's strategy with those discussed in this chapter (Alexander, Bradley, and Forbes).

5. Focusing on one event before the general election, such as a candidate debate, straw poll, or candidate forum at an interest-group or party-sponsored event, review the "morning after" press evaluation. Did the press cover all candidates equally? On what basis did the press luate candidates' performances and determine winners and losers?

6. Media exposés of the personal lives and private financial dealings of candidates play an increasingly important role in the campaign preliminaries. Is this type of reporting appropriate for the media? Does the public have the right to know all personal information about a candidate? If not, what kinds of information should be reported and what should not?

7. In the 2000 preliminaries at least two candidates, George W. Bush Jr. and Steve Forbes, did not accept public funding and therefore could spend an unlimited amount of money. In essence, there were two tiers of candidates in the pre–general election period: one group who had considerable financial support, did not need public funding, and as a result could spend unlimited amounts under present campaign finance law, and another group who had limited financial support, needed public funding, and as a result had to abide by state and national expenditure limits. Is this situation fair and does it need to be fixed? Discuss.

8. Many of the changes in the Democratic and Republican rules for selecting delegates have been rationalized on the basis of producing a "representative" convention and one that would nominate a potential winner. Review the changes in the rules over the past two decades, with the goal of identifying an ideal set of delegate selection rules that would produce both representative conventions and winners.

9. State parties and candidates themselves are challenging the national Republican and Democratic Parties for control of the rules of delegate selection. Who should have the power to establish these rules? Why? Explain.

10. Review the precise circumstances surrounding the withdrawal of candidates from the 2000 presidential campaign. List the characteristics of each situation and try to determine the role of money, caucus or primary results, adverse publicity, and other factors in their decision to end the campaigns.

11. Critics charge that only a select and unrepresentative sample of party members participate in caucuses, while a broader and more representative sample of party members participate in primaries. Is the primary system better than the caucus system? Do alternative methods exist that might be preferable?

12. Identify and evaluate the procedures for third parties or independent candidates to secure nomination for the general election ballot in your state.

Additional Sources

Printed Material and Videos

Ballot Access News. A monthly newsletter, published by the Coalition for Free and Open Elections, which focuses on state laws and judicial decisions that affect the access of minor parties and independent candidates to the ballot. Presenting a wealth of information as the election unfolds, from who is on the ballot in which states to updated information on the details of major and minor party nominating processes, this newsletter is an invaluable resource.

Broder, David. *Campaign for President: The Managers Look at '96.* Cambridge: John F. Kennedy School of Government, 1997. After every presidential campaign since 1972, the Kennedy School at Harvard University has invited major participants in the recently completed campaign to discuss it. This volume is the transcript of the latest discussion. If you can get beyond the egos involved, this is must reading, especially to understand pre–general election strategies. For students of any presidential election since 1972, the volume of proceedings for that election is also highly recommended.

Iowa Caucuses and *Republican Presidential Candidates Debate.* These two videos, available from C-SPAN Archives, focus on the 1996 Iowa caucuses. A look through the catalogue for other archived tapes from C-SPAN that deal with presidential election preliminaries is highly recommended.

Mayer, William G. "The Presidential Nominations." In *The Election of 1996*, ed. Gerald Pomper et al. Chatham, N.J.: Chatham House, 1997. A comprehensive and detailed look at the 1996 primaries and caucuses.

Orren, Gary R., and Nelson W. Polsby, eds. *Media and Momentum.* Chatham, N.J.: Chatham House, 1987. This volume contains five articles on many dimensions of the New Hampshire primary. Although a bit outdated, it remains one of the best print sources on this critical early delegate election event.

Sabato, Larry. "Presidential Nominations: The Front-loaded frenzy of '96." In *Toward the Millennium: The Elections of 1996,* ed. Larry Sabato. Boston: Allyn and Bacon, 1997. A review of the 1996 nomination process with interesting public opinion and voting trend data on a state-by-state basis. The book also contains insightful discussions of candidate strategies in the pre–general election campaign.

Online Data

Center for Responsive Politics. This is one of the most user-friendly campaign finance sites. A subsection aggregates and reorganizes presidential candidate data submitted to the FEC. If you want to look at the FEC data yourself, there are links to FEC reports. The center's newsletter, *Capital Eye,* focuses on topical campaign finance issues as they emerge.

To access: http://www.opensecrets.org/home/index.asp

CNN/All Politics. This site is CNN's online political news service. It is a must throughout the pre–general election process (and during the conventions and general election) for following all the candidates and their campaigns.

To access: http://www.cnn.com/ALLPOLITICS/index.html

Democracy in Action. This is one of the most comprehensive sites on the presidential selection process. Of particular note are subsections that discuss precampaign strategies of potential candidates and the delegate selection process. There is an individual review of each primary and caucus with relevant state demographic and party rules. What more could a primary and caucus maven want?

To access: http://gwu.edu/~action/P2000.html

DesMoines Register. This is the site of one of Iowa's major newspapers. For all the developments related to the Iowa caucuses, it is a critical source.

To access: http://dmregister.com/

The Federal Election Commission. This is the site of the government agency responsible (under the Federal Election Campaign Act) for monitoring campaigns and making all candidate and campaign financial reports available to the public. Although voluminous financial data are available on line, what is especially valuable is the commission's review of campaign finance law. See "Citizen's Guide to Contributions and the Law."

To access: http://www.fec.gov/

The Gallup Poll. The "politics and elections" section of the Gallup Organization's site reviews all recent polls on politics. During the primaries and caucuses, this will be a valuable source of data on the relative standing of the candidates.

To access: http://www.gallup.com/poll/index.asp

Politics1.com. One of the best sites on the presidential election process, this one provides links to dozens of declared and undeclared major and minor party candidates. It also offers a free daily newsletter.

To access: http://www.politics1.com/

WMUR-TV. This is the site of a New Hampshire television station. If anyone is going to cover the important minutiae of the state's primary, it will.

To access: http://www.wmur.com

Elizabeth Dole, Republican candidate for president in the 2000 election, was already well known to prospective voters from her husband's campaign in 1996. Here she mingles with delegates at the 1996 Republican National Convention in San Diego, breaking with normal convention protocol by leaving the podium to present her speech.

(Source: Win McNamee, Reuters)

3

Nomination

Although not all presidential candidates are formally nominated by conventions, the nominating conventions of the major parties still perform an important role for all nominees. Major party nominees rely on these gatherings for their formal nomination; in addition, the conventions are the first time they appear as candidates before a national audience. The conventions also give the candidates and parties an opportunity to create images and set themes, both positive and negative. Finally, the viability of third-party or independent candidates also remains closely tied to the dynamics of the major party conventions.

At a significant number of conventions in the past forty years, one clear choice for the nomination was accepted by virtually all segments of the party. This individual faced little or no opposition before the convention and was nominated on the first ballot. Franklin D. Roosevelt in 1936 and 1944, Dwight D. Eisenhower in 1956, Lyndon B. Johnson in 1964, Richard Nixon in 1972, Ronald Reagan in 1984, and Bill Clinton in 1996 are examples of such a candidate (see Tables 3-1, 3-2, and 3-3). In these cases, the other functions of the national nominating convention, such as fashioning a party platform and accrediting delegates, are generally performed with ease and little controversy. This unanimity has also narrowed the electoral opportunities for third parties or independent candidates.

Participants at major party conventions characterized by consensus, however, may squabble over matters that relate to future nominees. Because most of these conventions are nominating incumbent presidents for a second term, an unavoidable question is who will emerge as the heir apparent to the current chief executive? For example, at the 1956 and 1972 Republican conventions, the only matters of dispute related to the vice presidential nomination and the formula for allocating delegates for the next Republican convention. Each of these squabbles was the opening round for the 1960 and 1976 Republican nominations, respectively.

At the other extreme are party conventions at which presidential nominations are made only after intense ideological or factional conflict. In these cases, the nomination is hotly contested throughout the caucuses and primaries and occasionally (although not since 1952) resolved only after multiple convention ballots. Conflict pervades virtually every aspect of these conventions. These situations are made especially difficult when partisans in the struggles place more emphasis on their commitment to particular policy stands or to a particular candidate than on the nomination of a party standard-bearer who can win in November. One consequence of conventions with a significant level of unresolved conflict is that they increase the opportunities for third-party or independent candidates by prompting disgruntled major party members to support such candidacies.

Despite damaging public displays of rancor and intraparty discord, these conventions nonetheless were part of a presidential selection process in which conventions mattered—as decision-making bodies for the parties and as forums in which the nation was presented through television with its first and often enduring image of the candidate and the party. This is no longer the case. Major party nominations now are decided long before the conventions. Presumptive nominees, not the party, orchestrate the conventions. And the details of the party platform have disappeared into the background of convention hoopla, often to be ignored by the nominee. Commercial television networks have essentially abandoned the conventions, transforming what once was hours of coverage into a few minutes in prime time. In 1968 the three major networks aired a total of seventy-three hours of coverage of the major party nominating conventions. By 1984 that number had dropped to twenty-five. The ratings of even this limited coverage have declined (see Figure 3-1).

In sum, the nominating conventions matter less now because the major parties themselves are less at the center of the nominating process than at any time since conventions first developed in the early nineteenth century. Indeed, in a fundamentally new presidential selection process—in which the old political labels are not very meaningful, the public's identification with parties is declining, and candidates' image and style take precedence over party stances—the traditional nominating conventions likely will be altered significantly or will disappear altogether (see Figure 3-2).

Considerations for 2000

For both the Republican and Democratic Parties the 2000 nominating conventions present a tremendous challenge. Without issues that stir controversy or conflict, network television will have little interest in providing more than brief nightly coverage. The question is how can the parties produce the kind of story the media would relish without damaging their own public image? After all, a successful convention is one in which unanimity and enthusiasm are shown for the nominee and a positive theme or message is conveyed to the American people.

In 1996 the Democrats carefully planned a convention that would build toward the president's acceptance speech on the last evening. Recognizing that the media would focus on few of the other convention events or speeches, the president sought to attract coverage to his candidacy and platform in a 559-mile whistle-stop train tour through Appalachia and the Midwest. At each stop aboard "The Twenty-first Century Express," Bill Clinton unveiled a component of his platform to enthusiastic crowds. This clever strategy, however, was derailed at the last moment by a sex scandal involving Richard Morris, one of the president's closest advisers. In the end, the media's coverage of the scandal brought generally negative evaluations of the president during the Democratic convention: of all the comments about President Clinton aired on the network evening news programs during the convention, 61 percent were negative.

The overall goal for the Democrats at their 2000 convention is to highlight the accomplishments of the Clinton years while transcending the rancor and controversy associated with the impeachment of President Clinton. Accomplishing this would be no mean task for Vice President Al Gore if he wins the 2000 presidential nomination. Although Gore clearly cannot reject Clinton's support, he must distance himself from the president and develop a distinct and favorable identity. As the vice president emerged as a presidential candidate in early 1999, this challenge was made very clear in national polls. Clinton's mixed favorabilty ratings were a strong predictor of support for or opposition to Gore. A poll conducted in May 1999 by CNN, *USA Today,* and the Gallup Organization found that Clinton could be a major liability for Gore. Participants in the poll were asked, "Would you be more likely or less likely to vote for Al Gore for president if President Clinton were to actively support him and campaign for him?" Only 29 percent responded "more likely," while 52 percent said "less likely."

Further complicating this equation is the possibility that Hillary Rodham Clinton will run for a Senate seat in New York. Her candidacy would keep alive many of the controversies that arose during the Clinton administration. In sum, the Democrats need to fashion a convention that presents them as a party of notable domestic and international accomplishments during the Clinton years but one that is eager and ready to move forward unanimously with a new standard-bearer and agenda.

The challenge for the Republican Party is no less great. In 1996 the Republicans orchestrated their convention around the announcement of their vice presidential nominee, former representative Jack Kemp of New York, and a 15 percent tax cut as the core of their platform. At the convention, Elizabeth Dole, a former cabinet member and wife of Robert Dole, the presidential nominee, wowed the convention audience and the networks by breaking with the century-old tradition of formal speeches from the podium. Reminiscent of daytime television, she strolled through the audience, selectively introducing a series of guests who had played important roles in her husband's life. The speech was a clever move away from nineteenth-century oratory to a style more attuned to contemporary television. The networks were obviously pleased, staying with Mrs. Dole's speech after the hour break, even though they had scheduled commercial entertainment. Despite careful and successful planning, the Republican convention made little long-term difference in the presidential campaign. By the end of August, two weeks after the convention, the Dole-Kemp ticket trailed that of the Democrats by essentially the same margin as the week before the convention.

In 2000 the Republicans face a similar challenge. A well-orchestrated convention reflecting enthusiasm for the nominee may not interest the television networks or influence public opinion. Controversy and conflict, however, certainly will. And Republicans could well be faced with convention scenarios that would resemble a proverbial slug fest. The nomination of a centrist or undefined candidate, such as Elizabeth Dole or George Bush Jr., might prompt conservatives to insist on a platform or even a statement by the nominee affirming fundamental conservative positions. By the summer of 1999 conservatives in the party were already threatening to bolt as a result of frontrunner Bush's silence or compromise on social issues that were important to them.

Moreover, there is no guarantee that increased front loading in the selection of delegates will result in an early presumptive nominee firmly in control of the party before the convention. Indeed, high costs associated with campaigning in large and populous states that now select delegates simultaneously may make it impossible for any candidate, no matter how well funded, to secure an early nomination. In this regard, it is not impossible that the 2000 Republican proceedings could be the first in almost half a decade in which the nomination has not been decided before the convention. This development would certainly produce exciting television, but it may not be in the best interest of the party or the nominee.

The Reform Party also held a convention in 1996. Nominating Ross Perot for a second try for the presidency, the convention was noted more for its novelty than its relevance in the upcoming race. The two-part convention first met in Long Beach, California, and then reconvened in Valley Forge, Pennsylvania. A preliminary round of voting included anyone who signed a Reform Party petition or was enrolled in the party. Any candidate who got 10 percent of the vote could compete for the nomination at the first stage of the party's convention in Long Beach. After hearing speeches by the candidates, qualified voters could participate in the final selection by mail-in ballots, toll-free telephone numbers, or the Internet. In the end, the Reform convention was largely ignored by the media, receiving only eighteen minutes of network evening news time. Moreover, the innovative means of citizen participation in the proceedings failed, plagued by glitches and charges of bias and corruption. Only 5 percent of those eligible participated in the Reform Party nomination process.

The future of the Reform Party and its conventions depend to a large degree on the public's satisfaction with the nominees of the major parties. A revitalized Reform Party certainly does not lack potential candidates for 2000. Former professional wrestler Jesse Ventura was elected governor of Minnesota on the Reform ticket in 1998. However, in the end the success of the Democratic and Republican conventions matters more to the Reform Party than does its own.

It is no surprise, then, that the major parties spend considerable energy attempting to ensure that their conventions will receive wide and positive media coverage. These efforts include adjusting the convention schedule to network programming demands, distributing sound bites, providing video footage, and allowing live convention programming. Also a critical concern is choosing a site that can offer the most sophisticated facilities for radio, television, and now the Internet. In preparation for its 2000 convention in Philadelphia, Republicans chose the First Union Center because of its ultramodern communications infrastructure and facilities that would support cable television and continuous-feed radio for small stations as well as for network broadcasting. The Republicans also plan for the First Union Center to host their convention Web site, "PoliticalFest," which will feature interactive news, online conversations, news updates, and political exhibits.

Considerable planning and expense by both the Republicans and the Democrats, however, does not ensure that they can control the news that flows from the conventions. To a large degree, this is because national nominating conventions, despite their declining role in the selection of a presidential candidate, continue to pit party leaders and candidates attempting to control the public image of the proceedings against thousands of journalists who descend upon the convention searching for "news."

Points of Concern

Although presenting a positive image of convention proceedings to the public is important, conflict may appear at several critical points. First, if the nomination is still in doubt at the beginning of the convention, disputes over the rules that govern the proceedings and that can have a direct impact on the presidential nomination are possible. These rules deal with a wide range of matters, such as the length of debate on the convention floor, whether delegates can vote on issues that affect their own status at the convention, and whether presidential aspirants must announce a running mate before the balloting for president. At the 1980 Democratic convention, supporters of Massachusetts senator Edward M. Kennedy proposed that the rule requiring delegates to vote for the candidate to whom they were pledged be abolished (see Table 3-4). The change would have aided Kennedy, who was trailing President Jimmy Carter in pledged delegates.

Second, at closely contested conventions the accreditation of delegates may become an issue. For example, the challenge to the seating of certain delegates at the 1968 Democratic convention was closely related to the efforts of supporters of Sens. Eugene J. McCarthy of Minnesota and George McGovern of South Dakota to prevent the nomination of Vice President Hubert H. Humphrey. Similarly, the challenge to the seating of some delegates at the 1972 Democratic convention was related to tactical maneuvering by both pro-McGovern and anti-McGovern forces.

Third, the approval of a platform poses another potentially volatile scene when conventions are divided among factional and ideological rivals. Some intraparty differences over rival presidential aspirants represent deep divisions within the party over issues. In 1964, for example, the split within the Republican Party between supporters of Sen. Barry M. Goldwater of Arizona and anti-Goldwater forces was reflected early in the convention by a key vote over the platform plank on civil rights. In 1968 the split between Humphrey and anti-Humphrey forces at the Democratic convention mirrored differences over American policy in Vietnam. In this respect, the convention vote on the Vietnam plank of the platform was essentially a warm-up vote for the presidential nomination.

Finally, the nomination of a vice presidential candidate may reveal unresolved factional or ideological battles within the party. Since 1940, when Franklin D. Roosevelt handpicked his vice president, nominees for president have controlled the vice presidential nominating process, selecting running mates with whom they feel both personally and ideologically comfortable. The nomination for vice president, however, provides an opportunity for losing or disgruntled factions within the party to pursue at least some of their unfulfilled goals. Although vice presidential nominations of this sort generally are not much more than symbolic efforts, they can signal that the party has yet to achieve broad support for the presidential nominee or for the platform.

At best, a vice presidential nominee may soothe factional differences within the party, avert controversy, and ultimately aid the ticket by winning his or her home state. A significant number of recent vice presidential nominees have failed to meet even these far from rigorous requirements. In 1972 the Democratic candidate for vice president was forced to resign within two weeks of his nomination, following revelations that he had been hospitalized three times for "nervous exhaustion and fatigue." In 1984 and 1988 Democratic and Republican vice presidential nominees faced allegations of ethical improprieties. In 1992 Vice President Dan Quayle's support in public opinion polls was so low that President Bush seriously considered replacing him.

The nominating conventions of the major parties, therefore, reflect both a struggle for power within the party and an attempt to maintain, if not solidify, the coalitions that make up the party. Balancing these two goals is a difficult task made more sensitive because it occurs in public, under the watchful eyes of thousands of journalists. This situation is fraught with danger for the party and the nominee. As former Democratic National Committee chairman Robert Strauss once put it, conventions "are made for mischief."

Major Party Conventions: Media Events

Before a convention convenes, many of its basic features have been established by committees. In both the Republican and Democratic Parties these committees establish rules that govern the convention, accept credentials of the delegates, develop a party platform, and handle a myriad arrangements for the convention. Before presenting the recommendations of these committees, however, the convention has other business to perform. Initial events generally include welcoming speeches by officials from the host city and state, election of convention officers, reports from national party officials, speeches by party notables, and the convention's keynote address.

The keynote address is especially important because it sets the general tone of the convention—stressing the party's chosen themes and providing national exposure for the individual giving the address. Such exposure may further an already well developed national career or, indeed, may suddenly create one. For example, at the 1976 Democratic convention, keynote speaker Barbara Jordan received votes for both president and vice president—apparently the result of her dramatic address.

In a period of selective convention coverage by the television networks, the parties have a limited window of opportunity to reach a national audience. As a result, some changes in the structure of conventions have occurred. The parties now schedule during the day potentially divisive proceedings, mundane party business, and controversial speakers who cannot be denied the podium. Party notables and the nominees appear during the one or two hours of nightly network coverage. Although the keynote address has retained its traditional importance as one of these critical presentations, other prime-time speeches by party officials or notables can now have an equally defining national effect. In 1992, for example, several prime-time addresses at the Republican convention, including those by Patrick Buchanan and Marilyn Quayle, wife of the vice president, created a negative public image of the Republican convention and conveyed a strident tone, even though dozens of non–prime time speeches reflected a more low-keyed orientation.

Given the penchant of the networks to cover only events or speeches that would interest the broader public, the parties themselves have moved away from the purely political to schedule prime-time speakers whose personal stories would attract viewers. For the Democrats in 1996, this included Sarah Brady, wife of former Reagan press secretary James Brady, who was wounded in an attempted assassination of President Reagan, and Christopher Reeve, an actor who was paralyzed in an accident. The Republicans included AIDs activist Mary Fisher but did not schedule her in prime time.

Before the nomination of candidates, the convention generally reviews reports on party rules, acceptance of delegate credentials, and the party platform. Although the convention committees and the national party committees attempt to achieve consensus or compromise in all of these areas before the convention begins, that is not always possible. When a minimum number of delegates' signatures are secured (20 percent of the appropriate convention committee for the Democrats; 25 percent for the Republicans), both a majority report and minority positions are presented to the convention—a situation that can provide great drama for the mass media and give the impression of significant intraparty conflict to the public. Parties and prospective nominees therefore make great efforts to avoid or minimize such situations. In

1984, 1988, and 1992 the apparent Democratic nominees made a wide range of concessions to their vanquished opponents to avoid major floor fights at the upcoming conventions. In 1996 the Republican leadership made the platform process as short as possible to avoid scrutiny by the media of the inevitable debate over the plank on abortion. When an earlier agreement between Bob Dole, the presumptive nominee, and Rep. Henry Hyde, the platform committee chair, broke down, the platform continued to oppose abortion, while Dole's suggested language on tolerance of other positions on abortion was included in the appendix to the platform. This strategy ensured that the platform would pass quietly in committee and would receive routine approval on the floor of the convention. To the disappointment of the media, there was no discord in public over abortion.

Finally, the convention turns to what many view as its main business—the nomination of presidential and vice presidential candidates. Decisions about rules or credentials may already have determined the outcome of the nominating process, but the convention nonetheless moves through a ritual as old as the convention itself.

Candidates who have the minimal required number of delegate signatures are placed in nomination by prominent supporters, and a "spontaneous" demonstration of support ensues. (For the Democrats the required number is 300 delegates, with no more than 50 from any one state; for the Republicans the requirement is the majority of delegates in five states.) With the advent of television and the nominee's desire to address the greatest number of viewers possible, these spontaneous demonstrations have been curtailed. When convention events are not controlled, unfortunate consequences can result. For example, in 1972 Democratic nominee McGovern finally took the podium to give his acceptance speech at 2:48 a.m., far past prime-time television viewing.

Eventually the convention votes for the nominees on a state-by-state basis. In a close contest the voting process itself can generate considerable suspense. States may not vote when called, or they may stop the state-by-state polling because they are completing their tally. Additionally, when the result of the polling is obvious after all states have voted or have had the opportunity to vote, some states may change their votes. (This change is technically labeled a "shift.") The goal is to be part of the winning coalition.

The convention then moves to balloting for the vice presidential nomination. The presidential nominee selects the vice presidential nominee, who is virtually assured of receiving the nomination by a voting majority of delegates or by acclamation. However, exceptions to this rule exist. In 1956 Democratic nominee Adlai Stevenson decided to leave the choice to the convention. In the chaotic balloting that followed, a relatively unknown Massachusetts senator, John F. Kennedy, came just forty votes short of the vice presidential nomination.

The culmination of modern media conventions is the acceptance speeches of the presidential and vice presidential nominees. Nominees did not appear before the convention before 1932, when Franklin D. Roosevelt accepted the nomination in person, establishing the tradition among Democrats. Republican nominee Wendell Willkie began this practice among Republicans in 1940.

Just as prime-time speeches by party notables set the tone for the convention, the acceptance speech sets the tone for the upcoming campaign. Barry Goldwater, in accepting the 1964 Republican nomination, uttered perhaps the most prominent statement of the entire campaign: "And let me remind you that extremism in the defense of liberty is no vice. And let me remind you also that moderation in the pursuit of justice is no virtue."

In an age when sophisticated communications technology has made images and sounds as important as words, acceptance speeches become multidimensional presentations of the candidate to one of the largest audiences of the campaign. Whether the nominee can successfully communicate in this fashion is the first great test of his or her candidacy. In 1992 the Democrats mastered this challenge by concluding Clinton's acceptance speech with perhaps the convention's most telegenic moment: the presidential and vice presidential candidates dancing with their wives to Fleetwood Mac's "Don't Stop (Thinking about Tomorrow)."

After the acceptance speeches, the convention adjourns to prepare for the upcoming general election campaign, which traditionally has not begun until after Labor Day. Recently, however, candidates have been eager to hit the campaign trail immediately after the conventions. In both 1992 and 1996 nominees Clinton and Gore left the Democratic convention to tour the country. The goal in 1992 was to establish a populist tone for the campaign, while in 1996 it was to regain any momentum that had been lost during the sex scandal involving Dick Morris—the leading story of the 1996 Democratic convention. Despite such strategic adjustments, the conventions and the impressions they leave on the public have already set much of the groundwork for success or failure in November.

Table 3-1 Democratic Conventions, 1832–1996

Year	Location	Presidential nominee	Ballots
1832	Baltimore, Md.	Andrew Jackson	1
1835	Baltimore, Md.	Martin Van Buren	1
1840	Baltimore, Md.	Martin Van Buren	1
1844	Baltimore, Md.	James K. Polk	9
1848	Baltimore, Md.	Lewis Cass	4
1852	Baltimore, Md.	Franklin Pierce	49

Table 3-1 *Continued*

Year	Location	Presidential nominee	Ballots
1856	Cincinnati, Ohio	James Buchanan	17
1860	Charleston, S.C.	Deadlocked	57
	Baltimore, Md.	Stephen A. Douglas	2
1864	Chicago, Ill.	George B. McClellan	1
1868	New York, N.Y.	Horatio Seymour	22
1872	Baltimore, Md.	Horace Greeley	1
1876	St. Louis, Mo.	Samuel J. Tilden	2
1880	Cincinnati, Ohio	Winfield S. Hancock	2
1884	Chicago, Ill.	Grover Cleveland	2
1888	St. Louis, Mo.	Grover Cleveland	1
1892	Chicago, Ill.	Grover Cleveland	1
1896	Chicago, Ill.	William J. Bryan	5
1900	Kansas City, Mo.	William J. Bryan	1
1904	St. Louis, Mo.	Alton S. Parker	1
1908	Denver, Colo.	William J. Bryan	1
1912	Baltimore, Md.	Woodrow Wilson	46
1916	St. Louis, Mo.	Woodrow Wilson	1
1920	San Francisco, Calif.	James M. Cox	44
1924	New York, N.Y.	John W. Davis	103
1928	Houston, Texas	Alfred E. Smith	1
1932	Chicago, Ill.	Franklin D. Roosevelt	4
1936	Philadelphia, Pa.	Franklin D. Roosevelt	Acclamation
1940	Chicago, Ill.	Franklin D. Roosevelt	1
1944	Chicago, Ill.	Franklin D. Roosevelt	1
1948	Philadelphia, Pa.	Harry S. Truman	1
1952	Chicago, Ill.	Adlai E. Stevenson	3
1956	Chicago, Ill.	Adlai E. Stevenson	1
1960	Los Angeles, Calif.	John F. Kennedy	1
1964	Atlantic City, N.J.	Lyndon B. Johnson	Acclamation
1968	Chicago, Ill.	Hubert H. Humphrey	1
1972	Miami Beach, Fla.	George McGovern	1
1976	New York, N.Y.	Jimmy Carter	1
1980	New York, N.Y.	Jimmy Carter	1
1984	San Francisco, Calif.	Walter F. Mondale	1
1988	Atlanta, Ga.	Michael S. Dukakis	1
1992	New York, N.Y.	Bill Clinton	1
1996	Chicago, Ill.	Bill Clinton	1

Source: National Party Conventions, 1831–1996 (Washington, D.C.: Congressional Quarterly, 1997), 10.

Table 3-2 Republican Conventions, 1856–1996

Year	Location	Presidential nominee	Ballots
1856	Philadelphia, Pa.	John C. Fremont	2
1860	Chicago, Ill.	Abraham Lincoln	3
1864	Baltimore, Md.	Abraham Lincoln	1
1868	Chicago, Ill.	Ulysses S. Grant	1
1872	Philadelphia, Pa.	Ulysses S. Grant	1
1876	Cincinnati, Ohio	Rutherford B. Hayes	7
1880	Chicago, Ill.	James A. Garfield	36
1884	Chicago, Ill.	James G. Blaine	4
1888	Chicago, Ill.	Benjamin Harrison	8
1892	Minneapolis, Minn.	Benjamin Harrison	1
1896	St. Louis, Mo.	William McKinley	1
1900	Philadelphia, Pa.	William McKinley	1
1904	Chicago, Ill.	Theodore Roosevelt	1
1908	Chicago, Ill.	William H. Taft	1
1912	Chicago, Ill.	William H. Taft	1
1916	Chicago, Ill.	Charles E. Hughes	3
1920	Chicago, Ill.	Warren G. Harding	10
1924	Cleveland, Ohio	Calvin Coolidge	1
1928	Kansas City, Mo.	Herbert Hoover	1
1932	Chicago, Ill.	Herbert Hoover	1
1936	Cleveland, Ohio	Alfred M. Landon	1
1940	Philadelphia, Pa.	Wendell Willkie	6
1944	Chicago, Ill.	Thomas E. Dewey	1
1948	Philadelphia, Pa.	Thomas E. Dewey	3
1952	Chicago, Ill.	Dwight D. Eisenhower	1
1956	San Francisco, Calif.	Dwight D. Eisenhower	1
1960	Chicago, Ill.	Richard Nixon	1
1964	San Francisco, Calif.	Barry M. Goldwater	1
1968	Miami Beach, Fla.	Richard Nixon	1
1972	Miami Beach, Fla.	Richard Nixon	1
1976	Kansas City, Mo.	Gerald R. Ford	1
1980	Detroit, Mich.	Ronald Reagan	1
1984	Dallas, Texas	Ronald Reagan	1
1988	New Orleans, La.	George Bush	1
1992	Houston, Texas	George Bush	1
1996	San Diego, Calif.	Robert Dole	1

Source: National Party Conventions, 1831–1996 (Washington, D.C.: Congressional Quarterly, 1997), 12.

Table 3-3 First-Ballot Voting for Presidential Nominees at Democratic and Republican Conventions, 1972–1996

Convention	Votes needed to nominate	Presidential nominee	Votes received[a]
1972 Democratic	1,509	George McGovern	1,728
		Henry M. Jackson	525
		George C. Wallace	382
		Shirley Chisholm	152
		Terry Sanford	78
1972 Republican	675	Richard Nixon	1,347
		Pete McCloskey	1
1976 Democratic	1,505	Jimmy Carter	2,239
		Morris K. Udall	330
		Edmund G. Brown Jr.	301
		George C. Wallace	57
1976 Republican	1,130	Gerald R. Ford	1,187
		Ronald Reagan	1,070
1980 Democratic	1,666	Jimmy Carter	2,123
		Edward M. Kennedy	1,150
1980 Republican	998	Ronald Reagan	1,939
		John B. Anderson	37
		George Bush	13
1984 Democratic	1,967	Walter F. Mondale	2,191
		Gary Hart	1,201
		Jesse Jackson	466
1984 Republican	1,118	Ronald Reagan	2,233
1988 Democratic	2,082	Michael S. Dukakis	2,876
		Jesse Jackson	1,219
1988 Republican	1,140	George Bush	2,277
1992 Democratic	2,145	Bill Clinton	3,372
		Edmund G. Brown Jr.	596
		Paul Tsongas	209
1992 Republican	1,106	George Bush	2,166
		Patrick Buchanan	18
1996 Democratic	2,145	Bill Clinton	4,277
1996 Republican	996	Robert Dole	1,928
		Patrick Buchanan	43

Source: National Party Conventions, 1831–1996 (Washington, D.C.: Congressional Quarterly, 1997), 246–260.

[a] Fractional votes rounded to nearest whole number.

FIGURE 3-1   Television Audiences for Major Party Conventions, 1968–1996

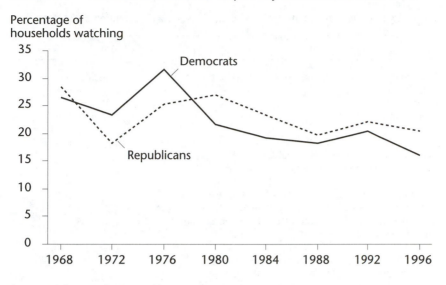

Percentage of
households watching

Source: Nielsen Media Research.

Note: The ratings for 1968–1988 are for the combined three-network (ABC, CBS, and NBC) average number of all TV households tuned in. For 1992 the rating is based on the five-network (ABC, CBS, NBC, CNN, and PBS) average number of TV households tuned in. For 1996 the Democratic convention rating is based on the five-network average number of all TV households tuned in, while the Republican convention rating is based on the six-network (ABC, CBS, NBC, CNN, PBS, and Family Channel) average. Data for 1968–1992 are for the percentage of TV households watching in an average minute during convention converage; 1996 data are for the percentage of TV households watching in an average minute during the final evening of convention coverage.

FIGURE 3-2   Voters Who Decided Their Vote During the Party Conventions, 1952–1996

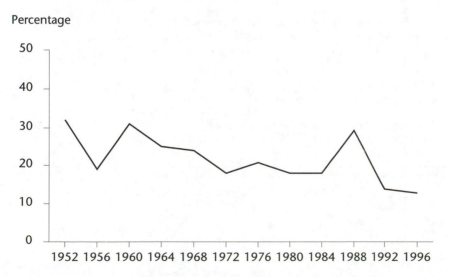

Percentage

Source: National Election Studies, Center for Political Studies, University of Michigan. Electronic resources from the NES World Wide Web site (www.umich.edu/~nes). Ann Arbor: University of Michigan, Center for Political Studies, 1995–1998.

Table 3-4 Prominent Rules, Credentials, and Platform Disputes at the National Convention, 1924–1996

Convention	Issue	Vote[a]
1924 Democratic	Formal opposition of the Democratic Party to the Ku Klux Klan	Yea, 542; nay, 543
1932 Republican	Repeal of Prohibition	Yea, 460; nay, 691
1948 Democratic	Amendment to platform statement on civil rights to include commendation of President Truman's civil rights program and support for congressional action in civil rights	Yea, 652; nay, 583
1952 Democratic	Seating of Virginia delegation despite its refusal to abide by earlier convention resolution requiring all delegates to work to place the national Democratic Party ticket on the ballot under the party's name in their state	Yea, 651; nay, 518
1964 Republican	Amendment to platform statement on civil rights to include specific pledges of speedy school desegregation, full voting rights, and the elimination of job discrimination	Yea, 409; nay, 897
1968 Democratic	Abolition of the unit rule	Yea, 1,351; nay, 1,209
	Amendment to platform statement on Vietnam to include a call for the immediate halt of the bombing of North Vietnam, reduction of offensive operations in South Vietnam, a negotiated troop withdrawal, and establishment of a coalition government in South Vietnam	Yea, 1,041; nay, 1,568
1972 Democratic	Seating of the California delegation despite its election by winner-take-all primary that was in violation of party rules	Yea, 1,618; nay, 1,238
1976 Republican	Requirement that all presidential candidates name their running mates prior to the convention vote for president	Yea, 1,069; nay, 1,180
1980 Democratic	Abolition of party rule binding delegates for one ballot to vote for candidates to whom they were pledged	Yea, 1,391; nay, 1,936
1984 Democratic	Abolition of dual primaries	Yea, 1,253; nay, 2,501
1988 Democratic	Amendment to platform pledging that the United States would make "no first use" of nuclear weapons	Yea, 1,221; nay, 2,474
1992 Democratic	Amendment to platform to delay a middle-class tax cut and a tax credit for families and children until the deficit was under control	Yea, 953; nay, 2,287

Source: National Party Conventions, 1831–1996 (Washington, D.C.: Congressional Quarterly, 1997).

[a] Fractional votes rounded to nearest whole number.

Table 3-5 Votes for African American Candidates at Major Party Conventions

Convention	Candidate	Office	Votes received[a]
1880 Republican	Blanche K. Bruce	Vice president	8
1888 Republican	Frederick Douglass	President	1
	Blanche K. Bruce	Vice president	11
1968 Democratic	Channing E. Phillips	President	68
	Julian Bond	Vice president	49
1968 Republican	Edward W. Brooke	Vice president	1
1972 Democratic	Shirley Chisholm	President	152
	Shirley Chisholm	Vice president	20
1976 Democratic	Barbara Jordan	President	1
	Ronald V. Dellums	Vice president	20
	Barbara Jordan	Vice president	28
1980 Democratic	Ronald V. Dellums	President	3
1984 Democratic	Jesse Jackson	President	466
	Shirley Chisholm	Vice president	39
1988 Democratic	Jesse Jackson	President	1,219
1992 Republican	Alan Keyes	President	1
1996 Republican	Alan Keyes	President	1

Sources: Richard C. Bain and Judith H. Parris, *Convention Decisions and Voting Records* (Washington, D.C.: Brookings Institution, 1973); *National Party Conventions, 1831–1996* (Washington, D.C.: Congressional Quarterly, 1997); and official proceedings of the Democratic and Republican conventions, 1880–1996.

[a] Fractional votes rounded to nearest whole number.

Table 3-6 Votes for Women Candidates at Major Party Conventions

Convention	Candidate	Office	Votes received[a]
1920 Democratic	Laura Clay	President	1
	Ella Stewart	President	1
	Annette Adams	President	1
1924 Democratic	Emma Miller	President	1
	Belle Miller	Presicent	1
	Lena Springs	Vice president	44
	Belle Miller	Vice president	3
	Maidee Renshaw	Vice president	3
	Margaret Chadbourne	Vice president	2
	Martha Bird	Vice president	1
1928 Democratic	Nellie Ross	Vice president	31
1964 Republican	Margaret C. Smith	President	27
1972 Democratic	Shirley Chisholm	President	152
	Frances Farenthold	Vice president	404
	Shirley Chisholm	Vice president	20
	Eleanor McGovern	Vice president	1
	Martha Griffiths	Vice president	1
1976 Democratic	Ellen McCormack	President	22
	Barbara Jordan	President	1
	Barbara Jordan	Vice president	28
1980 Democratic	Koryne Horbal	President	5
	Alice Tripp	President	2

Table 3-6 *Continued*

Convention	Candidate	Office	Votes received[a]
1980 Republican	Anne Armstrong	President	1
1984 Democratic	Martha Kirkland	President	1
	Shirley Chisholm	Vice president	39
	Geraldine A. Ferraro	Vice president	[b]
1984 Republican	Jeane J. Kirkpatrick	Vice president	1
1992 Democratic	Patricia Schroeder	President	8

Sources: Richard C. Bain and Judith H. Parris, *Convention Decisions and Voting Records* (Washington, D.C.: Brookings Institution, 1973); *National Party Conventions, 1831–1996* (Washington, D.C.: Congressional Quarterly, 1997); and official proceedings of the Democratic and Republican conventions, 1996.

[a] Fractional vote rounded to nearest whole number.
[b] Nominated by acclamation.

Table 3-7 Characteristics of Convention Delegates, Party Members, and the General Public, 1996

Characteristic	Democratic delegates	Democratic voters	All voters	Republican voters	Republican delegates
Gender					
Men	50%	42%	49%	53%	64%
Women	50	58	51	47	36
Race/ethnicity					
White	67	73	84	95	91
Black	19	21	10	2	3
Hispanic	9	7	5	2	3
Age					
Median (in years)	49	46	46	44	52
Education					
College graduate	68	19	24	30	73
Religion					
Protestant	47	59	59	64	62
Catholic	30	24	24	22	25
Jewish	6	3	2	—[a]	3
Evangelical/ born-again	13	22	24	31	31
Ideology					
Liberal	43	27	16	7	—[a]
Moderate	48	54	47	40	27
Conservative	5	17	34	50	70
Opinions					
Government should do more to solve the nation's problems	76	40	35	18	4
Government should do more to promote traditional values	27	46	42	44	56

Table 3-7   *Continued*

Characteristic	Democratic delegates	Democratic voters	All voters	Republican voters	Republican delegates
Organized prayer should be permitted in public schools	20	66	66	69	57

Source: CBS News/*New York Times* delegate surveys.

[a] Less than 1 percent.

Exercises

1. Since 1956 both major parties have needed only one ballot at their national conventions to nominate a presidential candidate. Some commentators say that future multiballot conventions are unlikely because of biases in the press, the campaign finance system, and the delegate selection schedule that favors front-runners. Discuss how close the major party conventions in 2000 came to multiple ballots and outline the factors that potentially could produce that outcome.

2. Credentials, rules, or platform fights often are directly related to the struggle for the nomination at major party conventions. Indeed, the votes frequently serve as accurate predictors of the presidential balloting.

Using information in this chapter, select a convention and compare the vote on a particular credentials, rules, or platform fight to the first-ballot vote for presidential nominees. How do the two votes relate?

3. Review the 2000 Democratic and Republican conventions. With an eye toward a successful general election campaign, list positive and negative developments at each convention.

4. Review the media coverage of the 2000 Democratic and Republican conventions. Identify themes presented by the coverage. Did these themes present positive or negative images of the proceedings? In general, what did this coverage emphasize and what did it ignore? Did

media emphasis help, hurt, or have no effect on public perceptions of the nominees and their parties?

5. Both the Democrats and the Republicans had Internet sites at their conventions. What difference did they make?

6. What was the effect of the major party conventions on potential or declared independent or third-party candidates in 2000? Did the conventions help or hurt these candidates? How?

7. You are a top aide to either the Republican or Democratic presumptive nominee. Write a memo outlining the organization and presentation of the upcoming convention. The memo should deal with such items as credentials, rules, or platform concessions that might be appropriate; the selection of a vice presidential nominee; prime-time speakers; the substance and style of the nominee's acceptance speech; and a general strategy to deal with the media.

8. Organize a debate on the pros and cons of major party national nominating conventions. Do they still serve critical functions, or are they outdated and unnecessary?

9. Compare a nineteenth-century national nominating convention to one in the past decade. How many of the differences can be explained by the development of sophisticated electronic media?

10. Support for African American and women presidential or vice presidential candi-

dates at major party nominating conventions has been minimal since the 1980s (see Tables 3-5 and 3-6). Will 2000 be different? In answering this question, explain the dynamics in each major party that encourage or discourage African American or women candidates.

11. In 1996 the delegates to both major party conventions were not representative of party members as a whole (see Table 3-7). For example, Democratic delegates were substantially more liberal than party members as a whole, while Republican delegates were much more conservative than party members as a whole.

Does this discrepancy matter? Is it worthwhile to pursue a goal of conventions that are not only ideologically representative but also identical to overall party membership in terms of gender, age, and class? Why? Is such a convention possible?

12. Identify a potential or declared independent or third-party candidate and examine how that candidate gains access to the general election ballot in your state. Evaluate this process in your state. Is it onerous or just about right?

Additional Sources

Printed Material and Videos

Bain, Richard et al. *The Politics of National Party Conventions*. Washington, D.C.: Brookings Institution, 1960. Perhaps the most comprehensive study to date of convention organization and decision making through the 1950s.

National Party Conventions, 1831–1996. Washington, D.C.: Congressional Quarterly, 1997. The latest edition of this valuable review of convention history. The volume includes narrative descriptions of all major party conventions and key nomination and platform votes.

1996 Democratic Convention Highlights and *1996 Republican Convention Highlights*. These videos, available from C-SPAN Archives, contain major speeches and pro-ceedings of the Republican and Democratic conventions.

Sautter, R. Craig, and Edward M. Burke. *Inside the Wigwam: Chicago Presidential Conventions, 1860–1996*. Chicago: Wild Onion Books, 1996. Prepared in conjunction with the 1996 Democratic convention, this book remains an enlightening source of information on all twenty-five national party nominating conventions held in Chicago.

Splaine, John. *The Road to the White House since Television*. Washington, D.C.: C-SPAN, 1995. A review of every presidential election from 1949 through 1992, with an emphasis on the role of television. Each chapter contains useful and interesting information on television at the party nominating conventions. Did you know that President Truman was barely visible to the 1948 television audience when he gave his acceptance speech because he wore a white summer suit?

Online Data

Democracy in Action. This site has a brief but insightful review of nominating conventions and many great links to other convention-related sites.

To access: http://gwu.edu/~action/P2000.html

Democratic National Committee. As the nominating season progresses, the DNC's official site will have details of the Democratic convention and links to the convention's Web site.

To access: http://www.democrats.org/index.html

Life at the Conventions. This is the site of *Life* magazine, which provides fifty photos from conventions since 1948.

To access: http://www.pathfinder.com/Life/conventions/

Princeton University Deployable Video Library. This site provides access to sixty-nine videos. Users have the option of viewing boards of the item or seeing a video presentation with sound. Included are old Universal newsreels of the 1932 Democratic convention.

To access: http://www.videolib. princeton.edu/contents.html

Republican National Committee. The RNC's new Web site specializes in Republican news and information. Ultimately it should contain considerable information about the Republican convention and provide links to the convention's Web site.

To access: http://www.rnc.org/

Republican nominee Bob Dole (left) and President Bill Clinton (right) face off between moderator Jim Lehrer in the first of the presidential debates on October 6, 1996. Presidential and vice-presidential debates often raise new issues or reinforce lingering public perceptions, from Lloyd Bentsen's withering "you're no Jack Kennedy" response to VP nominee Dan Quayle, to Dole's pointed references to Clinton's war record.

(Source: Gary Hershorn, Reuters)

4

The Campaign Trail

General election campaigns for president historically have been rooted in two fundamental and strategic facts: these elections actually are won in an obscure body called the electoral college, and most Americans are motivated on election day by their attachment to one of the major political parties. The ongoing transformation of the presidential selection process, however, is rapidly changing the relevance and importance of both of these factors, and in the process it is redirecting campaign strategies.

The Electoral College

American presidential elections are not national elections in which the candidate receiving the most popular votes wins. National popular votes are neither the basis upon which the votes in American presidential elections are counted nor the basis upon which the campaigns are conducted.

Presidents normally win an election by obtaining a majority (270) of the 538 electoral votes. Almost all states allocate their total electoral votes to the candidate who receives more popular votes on a statewide basis than any other candidate. (The two exceptions, Maine and Nebraska, allot their electoral votes on both a congressional district and a statewide basis.) Each state's electoral votes equal its combined number of senators and representatives. Thus

popular victories in large states, even by the narrowest of margins, become critical to a successful campaign. For example, winning California by one popular vote, and thereby receiving its fifty-four electoral votes, makes up for losing by tens of thousands of popular votes in the states of Alaska, Arizona, Hawaii, Idaho, Montana, Nevada, Oregon, Utah, Washington, and Wyoming.

As a result, the arithmetic of the electoral college has focused presidential elections on a small number of populous states. Not surprisingly, since 1968 all successful presidential candidates have won popular vote victories in, and thereby received all the electoral votes of, at least half of the following states: California, Florida, Illinois, Michigan, New Jersey, New York, Ohio, Pennsylvania, and Texas (see Tables 4-1 and 4-2).

This bias in the electoral college was good news for the Republicans for two decades. In the six presidential elections from 1968 to 1988, Republican presidential candidates regularly won the electoral votes of six of the nine critical states. Moreover, in these six elections they won all the electoral votes in eighteen smaller states, primarily in the West and Midwest. As a result, some election analysts concluded that Republicans had a "lock" on the electoral college that Democrats had little hope of picking. The 1992 and 1996 elections changed this prognosis (see Table 4-3).

In both 1992 and 1996 the Democrats were able to attain substantial electoral college majorities through popular vote victories in the far West and Northeast. This new coalition was remarkably stable, with twenty-nine states and the District of Columbia voting Democratic in both elections. Only five states switched from the Democrats to the Republicans, or vice versa, during this period.

Although these two victories reflect some short-term stability in a new Democratic coalition under President Bill Clinton, they also reflect considerable electoral flux and shifting of voter loyalties. Third-party presidential candidates did better in 1992 and 1996 than in any other successive presidential elections in this century. In fact, independent and third-party candidacies in 1992 and 1996 came very close to altering the way the electoral college directs overall candidate strategies.

In a general election in which the two major parties face little competition from third parties or independents, their respective campaigns focus only on states in which the expenditure of resources can make a difference in producing a popular vote plurality. Why expend resources on a state in which you will already win or lose all the electoral votes? In this regard, the winner-take-all feature of the electoral college directs candidates and the campaigns to large, competitive states. In a three- or four-candidate race, however, campaign strategies would be quite different. If an electoral college majority might not be attainable, candidates would be forced to gear their campaigns toward the possibility of the House of Representatives selecting the president. Campaigns would be run with the ultimate goal of influencing members of Congress, who on a state-by-state basis would select the president.

Because there are no established criteria governing how members of Congress should vote in such an event, presidential candidates and campaigns would enter an uncharted area of electoral politics. It is clear, however, that in multicandidate presidential races, campaigns would focus on smaller and more selective segments of the voting population, since only a bare plurality of the vote would be necessary to secure all of the electoral votes for a particular state. In such races, nominees would not necessarily be forced to build broad coalitions of support or wage a national campaign.

Although this scenario may appear far-fetched, the early competition in 1992 among incumbent president George Bush, Bill Clinton, and Ross Perot, showing each with about a third of the popular vote, sent Congress scurrying for precedents to guide them in selecting a president if the electoral college failed to do so.

Partisanship

The second important, but often ignored fact about U.S. presidential elections, is that voter behavior in the general election is explained significantly by partisan affinities. Voters' attachment to one of the two major parties has provided an enduring context in which elections are fought and campaigns pursued. "If," as Thomas Patterson has eloquently stated, "the campaign is to be a time for the voters to exercise their discretion, they need help in discovering what their choices represent." This help is provided primarily by political parties.

Although partisanship is still one of the major motivators for political participation and one of the best indicators of voter choice, it has become less of an overall guide for voters in recent years. Partisans are increasingly dissatisfied with their party's nominees, and there are a growing number of independents, who make choices among candidates largely devoid of partisan considerations.

The waning influence of partisanship is seen in a number of ways. First, voters say they are dissatisfied with their electoral choices. Since July 1994 almost half of all respondents in polls conducted by the Pew Research Center have agreed that "we should have a third major political party in this country in addition to the Democrats and Republicans." Second, partisanship as a broad perceptual screen, which motivates citizens to vote for the nominees of their party at all levels of government and to participate in politics, now exerts much less influence on election day than it did in the past. In every presidential election since 1968 more than one-quarter of the voters have supported a presidential candidate of one party and the candidate of another party for the House of Representatives (see Table 4-4). Until then, this kind of electoral behavior had been rare, and when it existed it generally reflected a drastic change or "realignment" in citizen attachments to the two major parties.

The number of voters who consider themselves independents has also risen significantly, now approximating about the same proportion of the electorate as Democrats or Republicans. Not only are independents less likely to vote than are those who identify with a party, but when they do enter the electoral arena, they are more likely to support independent or third-party candidates or split their votes among the major party candidates. For example, only 4 percent of Democrats and 5 percent of Republicans supported Reform Party candidate Ross Perot in 1996, while 19 percent of independents supported him. Not surprisingly, 90 percent of all Democrats voted for President Clinton, 85 percent of all Republicans voted for former senator Robert Dole, and independents split 48 percent for Clinton and 33 percent for Dole (see Table 4-5).

Clearly, other factors have always modified the role partisanship plays in presidential elections. Also influencing a voter's decision are the perceived personality traits and attributes of the candidates as well as the policy preferences of the voter. A voter's perception of a presidential candidate's basic skills and qualities is an increasingly important consideration that may modify, if not neutralize, the impact of partisanship. Is the candidate knowledgeable about particular issues? Could the candidate solve particular problems? If elected, would the candidate provide strong leadership? In general, is the candidate honest and trustworthy? This last question emerged as a poten-

tially important one for voters in 1996, as the Whitewater investigation of President Clinton and his associates unfolded. Despite the fact that 54 percent of all voters and 20 percent of Clinton voters said they did not think the president was trustworthy and honest, other considerations prevailed in the voting booth. For example, 89 percent of voters who felt that the most important quality in a candidate was to be "in touch with the 1990s" voted for Clinton. Of those who felt the most important quality was "a vision for the future," 77 percent voted for the president (see Table 4-6).

The second factor modifying voter partisanship involves policy positions. When voters can identify their own positions with those of the candidates, strong policy voting takes place. In the 1992 election, for example, data collected by the National Election Studies of the University of Michigan and analyzed by Robert S. Erikson and Kent L. Tedin reveal a strong relationship between voters' positions on economic and foreign policy issues and their votes. Of voters who took the most liberal stances on ten economic and foreign policy issues, 92 percent voted for Clinton, while 85 percent of those who took the most conservative stances voted for President Bush. Even though only a minority of voters view elections in these terms, many others may cast ballots in a more general sense on the basis of issues. Voters may not refer to this match or mismatch of policy preferences, but they may speak of the party or candidate that best represents people like them.

Broad categories of voter self-identification, such as social class, religion, gender, or race, may also affect voting decisions. The greater the intensity and importance of these affiliations, the greater their impact in establishing a stable voter identity. African Americans as a group possess a predictable and identifiable partisanship and perspective on many policy issues. There is also evidence that women have a somewhat distinct perspective on many policy issues. Most recently, Democratic presidential candidates have done much better among women than among men because women are less conservative than men and are more favorably inclined toward a role for the federal government, especially in social policy areas. Republicans are currently speculating whether Elizabeth Dole on the ticket could reverse this trend by retaining moderate Republican women and attracting substantial numbers of Democratic women. The selection of a woman or Hispanic as the vice presidential nominee by the Democratic presidential nominee would also be gauged to hold or secure the votes of these groups within the electorate.

Candidate Strategies

To win the general election, candidates must develop strategies based on party affiliation, voters' perspectives on the skills and qualities of all the candidates, and voters' perceptions of the policy preferences of the candidates. Candidates must hold their own core partisan constituency and attract enough undecided voters to build a state-by-state majority in the electoral college. These strategies involve emphasizing the strengths of the candidate and exploiting the weaknesses of the opposition.

In the 1996 general election the Democratic and Republican strategies emphasized somewhat different issues. S. Robert Lichter and Richard E. Noyes reviewed for the Markle Foundation 270 campaign speeches and more than 400 television commercials produced by each campaign and the national party committees. Their findings revealed that the Clinton campaign emphasized education, children, and the economy, while the Dole campaign focused on taxes, drug abuse, the economy, Medicare, and President Clinton's honesty. Despite millions of dollars spent to sway voters, the 1996 general election campaign apparently mattered very little. In a national survey conducted by the *Washington Post,* Harvard University, and the Henry J. Kaiser Family Foundation, seven in ten voters said they had chosen a candidate either before or during the two parties' national conventions. Additionally, the survey found that citizens' knowledge of the major candidates did not increase during the general campaign. Indeed, the 1996 general election campaign reflected remarkably little change in the overall standing of the candidates from September until election day (see Figure 4-1).

It is not completely clear why the 1996 campaign changed few votes, but there are several new variables in 2000 that could increase the importance of the general election campaign. First, none of the likely candidates has the name recognition or visibility among the public of President Clinton or Senator Dole, the 1996 major party nominees. In the 2000 general election the probable nominees—Vice President Gore or former senator Bill Bradley for the Democrats and George Bush Jr. for the Republicans—are much less well known commodities than their 1996 counterparts. In this regard, there is more opportunity for both the candidates and the campaigns to define the election for the public. Moreover, the 2000 campaign will be the first in more than a century to take place immediately after the impeachment of a president. Although the media quickly moved on after President Clinton was acquitted, it is unclear how this event will affect the 2000 general election. What did the public conclude from the impeachment episode, and how will it affect voters' predisposition toward particular candidates or parties? The majority of the public opposed both impeachment and conviction, but is there nonetheless a "Clinton fatigue" among voters that will play out in the selection of candidates in the general election?

In 2000 the Democratic campaign will attempt to mobilize traditional Democrats, who are generally somewhat liberal in orientation, and independents, who are more moderate. Because this coalition was created and held together by President Clinton, the critical question for 2000 is whether another Democratic candidate can succeed in maintaining it. To a large degree, Democratic success rests on the party's ability to hold the center and not be portrayed as too far to the left. Although Clinton did a superb job in positioning the party on such issues as the budget, gun control, education, and welfare reform, it is unclear whether a successor can as adeptly follow this course and not be burdened by the ethical baggage left by his predecessor.

Republicans face an equally challenging task in the 2000 general election. President Clinton's movement to the center means that Republicans have "lost" many issues that they traditionally claimed. In this regard, they need to reinvent themselves and forge a general election strategy that holds their generally conservative partisans and attracts moderates. This coalition building may well be more difficult for Republicans than for Democrats in 2000. The early reaction of some Republican partisans to the candidacies of Elizabeth Dole and George Bush Jr. suggests the difficulty any GOP standard-bearer would have in moving to the middle on issues such as abortion and gun control. Without this kind of compromise, however, is unclear whether the ethical lapses of the Clinton administration would be enough to elect a Republican on election day.

With these dynamics, third-party or independent challenges in the 2000 general election are likely from the conservative end of the political spectrum. Although Perot's candidacies in 1992 and 1996 drew voters from both major parties and across the ideological spectrum, a third-party challenge from the right would disproportionately siphon off Republican votes. The early defection of Sen. Robert Smith of New Hampshire from the Republican race to seek the nomination as an independent or third-party candidate has already raised this specter for the Republicans. A more ill defined Reform Party candidacy of the middle also should not be discounted for election 2000, especially since the Reform Party's performance in 1996 again assures its nominee of partial public funding in the general election.

Whether specific campaign strategies are successful hinges on the ability of the respective campaigns to control the terms of debate and thereby alter voter perspectives in their favor. In this regard, the general election campaign may be viewed as a series of planned and unplanned events that influence voter perspectives and ultimately guide voter behavior on election day. But, most important, it is an exercise in working the media to best advantage.

The Role of the Mass Media

The primacy of partisanship in presidential elections logically corresponded with the dominance of political parties in American politics. Parties reinforced partisan behavior by controlling the content and distribution of political information to citizens. Party decline is a complex and multifaceted phenomenon. One critical part of this change has been the development of independent media that dominate the flow of information about candidates, campaigns, and the general political process. It is this new role for the media that best explains contemporary trends in voter behavior and candidate strategies.

Voters now receive most of their information about candidates and the campaign through mass media that are oriented toward human interest stories of conflict and travail, centered on an individual episode. The media have become journalist centered: more time and space are spent on journalists' interpretations of events than on the words or deeds of newsmakers. This approach to the news has consequences for media coverage of elections.

The preferred election story follows who is up or down in the race, covers conflict within or between campaigns, or digs into the personal travails of a candidate. Less information is conveyed about policy issues than in years past, and the general tone of most stories is negative. Stories are conveyed to the audience primarily by a notable journalist, with fewer than ten seconds provided for quotes or "bites" from the candidates or their spokespersons. Good visuals are a requirement of each story.

In 1996 this media bias was clear. A study by the Center for Media and Public Affairs of 483 network evening news stories from Labor Day to election day found that 48 percent focused on "horse race" or strategic themes and pretty much ignored Perot, who was seen as having no chance to win and therefore was not part of the strategic equation (see Table 4-7). Coverage of Dole, and what little attention was given to Perot was largely negative, while that of Clinton was equally divided. The nation's premier news magazines, such as *Time* and *Newsweek,* also reflected a generally negative attitude toward the candidates. Thirty years ago it would have been difficult to find any news magazine stories critical of major party candidates, but their 1996 campaign coverage included articles with saucy titles such as "Bob and Bill's Beltway Bake-Off" or "Peering through the Smoke," replete with derisive cartoons. Candidates rarely spoke for themselves on the network news but were interpreted by the media. Indeed, general election coverage in 1996, as in 1992, was much more about the press than the candidates. Prime-time viewers were six times as likely to hear talk from anchors or reporters than from the candidates themselves.

This type of coverage correlates with declining voter knowledge of policy issues and with increased negative perspectives toward all candidates and government in general. Additionally, the media have been unable to generate the levels of voter interest and participation once routinely facilitated by strong political parties and voters' sense of partisanship.

Candidates and campaigns have been forced to operate within the new and developing rules of media coverage; they must make "news" according to the media's own criteria. This includes not only conforming to what the media consider the appropriate substance of news but also to its visual standards. Whether a campaign can do this week after week in the general election is a prerequisite to its success. Media coverage of the major campaigns during the second week of September 1996 is a good example of how candidates must adapt or lose control of their campaigns.

Early in the week President Clinton stood at the Grand Canyon to dedicate the red rock canyons of Utah as a national monument. Not only did this stunning visual convey more about Clinton's concern about the environment than any speech, but the president was joined by actor Robert Redford. Star power plus an exquisite background framed the message. Later in the week the president received the endorsement of the nation's largest police union. Appearing before a sea of blue uniforms, Clinton visually appropriated what formerly had been a Republican issue—law and order.

If the Democratic campaign successfully navigated the national media that week, the Republican campaign did not. In California, Dole attacked the morals of the Hollywood entertainment industry. And, although most Americans probably agreed with him, the visuals that accompanied the speech were unremarkable. Even more problematic that week for the Republican campaign was Dole's fall from a podium in Chico, California, when a railing gave way. Dole was uninjured and gave his speech, but the news photo of a grimacing Dole lying on the ground—not the text of the candidate's speech—conveyed the Republican campaign message that week: Dole was too old and frail for the presidency.

Incumbent presidents running for reelection, of course, have an advantage in terms of their access to the media. News making is one of the perks of office. President Clinton's central role in pursuing peace in the Middle East and fostering a tolerable resolution of conflicts in volatile areas of the world provided abundant publicity advantages over his campaign rivals. The president also can gain positive publicity through his role in setting the nation's legislative agenda. President Bush's April 1991 announcement of proposed reforms in the public school system not only confronted a national problem but also served to protect Bush from charges of weak leadership on the domestic front. President Clinton's unveiling in June 1995 of his plan for a balanced budget gave him the opportunity to reposition himself against his Republican opposition. Vice presidents running for the presidency also can have similar advantages. With the cooperation of President Clinton, Vice President Gore, for example, can be placed in visible and very public roles related to both domestic and foreign policy.

Even when candidates and campaigns are mindful of the contemporary requirements of positive coverage by the media, the best-laid media strategy can go awry. In May 1996 Dole resigned his seat in the Senate, where he was majority leader, to be able to devote more time to his presidential campaign. Although the media's initial reaction to this announcement was positive, what Dole did, in effect, was to relinquish his role as a legislative newsmaker and assume that of a candidate who had the burden of making news. As campaign coverage dwindled, this strategy turned out to be questionable.

Unplanned events can also damage campaigns or spin them out of control. Most common are discrete campaign episodes that raise new issues or reinforce old ones. Dole's fall from the platform is only the most recent example. Republican nominee Dan Quayle's lackluster performance during the 1988 vice presidential debate reinforced widespread public perceptions that he was not qualified for office. In 1992 and 1996 the series of alleged improprieties related to Governor and then President Clinton's private life and personal financial dealings constantly underscored "character" as a potential campaign issue. Of a much larger magnitude are economic or international events that occur during the general election campaign. These can persuade voters that either a change or continuity is necessary. In 1956 the Suez crisis sealed the fate of an already struggling Democratic campaign by convincing many voters that it was an inopportune time to change administrations. Conversely, the lingering Iranian hostage situation in 1980 provided daily reminders of the foreign policy failures of Jimmy Carter's presidency and convinced many voters that change was critical.

The increasing dominance of an independent media in defining the terms of presidential campaigns and of political discourse in general has led candidates to look for ways in which they can regain control of their messages to the public. The recent developments of alternative media formats in television and radio and new communications technologies have accelerated this search. In essence, candidates now have new opportunities to communicate with the public and circumvent the nightly network news.

In the 1992 campaign this change was reflected in the candidates' emphasis on nontraditional news formats. These formats often provided direct interaction between candidate and audience, thus lessening the potential role of the journalist or host in structuring the "news" in a way that might be unfavorable or unflattering to the candidate. Perot declared his candidacy on *Larry King Live,* while Clinton wore dark glasses and played the saxophone as he introduced himself to the American public on the *Arsenio Hall Show*. Indeed, some labeled the 1992 election the "Talk Show Campaign."

For the 1996 campaign, the rapid development of the Internet made a new kind of communication between candidates and their supporters feasible at an acceptable cost. And although only 6–10 percent of the public went to a Web site to obtain political information during the campaign, it was clear that the Internet held great potential for dispensing information, raising funds, and organizing supporters. The successful 1998 gubernatorial campaign of former professional wrestler Jesse Ventura, who used the Internet as his primary organizing tool in an underfunded, understaffed, third-party candidacy in Minnesota, further suggested to candidates and campaigns that at long last it might be possible to circumvent the traditional media. The Internet, however, like all forms of communication, contains biases in terms of how it conveys information and who uses its. Its impact on the general election is one of the important unanswered questions of the latest presidential selection cycle.

Election 2000 already reflects candidates' efforts to circumvent media bias. One Republican declared his candidacy on line. All presidential candidates will soon be able to raise money on line through the use of credit cards. The 2000 election will be the first election in which candidates can advertise on line to targeted lists of voters. The talk show circuit has become a regular feature of candidates' behavior. Another Republican candidate announced his candidacy on *Larry King Live,* and on the day of his formal announcement Vice President Gore discussed his presidential bid with television journalist Diane Sawyer on ABC's *20/20* news magazine show. Typical of the contemporary media context of elections, ABC gave almost equal billing to journalist Sawyer and candidate Gore. According to the ads, "Diane Sawyer goes one on one with Al Gore."

In sum, the mass media continue to set the general context of a presidential election. But changes in the media have also created new opportunities for candidates. Indeed, successful candidates, like successful politicians in general, are often those who are most adept at innovation within the rapidly changing world of telecommunications. Just as President Franklin Roosevelt pioneered the political use of radio during the 1932 and 1936 presidential campaigns and Sen. Richard M. Nixon used television to save his place on the 1952 Republican ticket, success in 2000 may well depend on one of the nominees emerging as the latest innovator amidst rapid change in communications technology.

Another rapidly changing constraint for presidential candidates relates to money. On the basis of the 1996 election returns, Democratic and Republican Party nominees qualify for full public funding, and the Reform Party candidate qualifies for partial funding. Democratic or Republican nominees who wish to accept full funding will have a cap on expenditures. And although there are ever widening loopholes that allow candidates, campaigns, and the national parties to circumvent this cap, the emphasis of contemporary presidential elections on the mass media make campaigns very expensive. In particular, the high cost of prime-time advertising forces candidates to make choices about which voters and media markets to target. This will also be the case for self-financed general election campaigns that would not be subject under the law to any expenditure limits. Clinton's campaign developed a formula to help make these difficult media decisions and in the process coined a new election phrase—"cost per persuadable voter."

Beyond working within and around the constantly changing strategic constraints, a successful general election campaign may hinge on little more than luck. One wonders, for example, what the 1980 election results would have been if President Carter had been able to retrieve the American hostages from Iran shortly before the election, or what the dynamics of the 1996 general election would have been if Monica Lewinsky had been discovered before, not after, the election.

Table 4-1 State-by-State Electoral College Vote, 1968–1996

State	1996 Electoral votes	Winning party							
		1968	1972	1976	1980	1984	1988	1992	1996
Alabama	9	AI	R	D	R	R	R	R	R
Alaska	3	R	R	R	R	R	R	R	R
Arizona	8	R	R	R	R	R	R	R	D
Arkansas	6	AI	R	D	R	R	R	D	D
California	54	R	R	R	R	R	R	D	D
Colorado	8	R	R	R	R	R	R	D	R

Table 4-1 *Continued*

State	1996 Electoral votes	Winning party							
		1968	1972	1976	1980	1984	1988	1992	1996
Connecticut	8	D	R	R	R	R	R	D	D
Delaware	3	R	R	D	R	R	R	D	D
District of Columbia	3	D	D	D	D	D	D	D	D
Florida	25	R	R	D	R	R	R	R	D
Georgia	13	AI	R	D	D	R	R	D	R
Hawaii	4	D	R	D	D	R	D	D	D
Idaho	4	R	R	R	R	R	R	R	R
Illinois	22	R	R	R	R	R	R	D	D
Indiana	12	R	R	R	R	R	R	R	R
Iowa	7	R	R	R	R	R	D	D	D
Kansas	6	R	R	R	R	R	R	R	R
Kentucky	8	R	R	D	R	R	R	D	D
Louisiana	9	AI	R	D	R	R	R	D	D
Maine	4	D	R	R	R	R	R	D	D
Maryland	10	D	R	D	D	R	R	D	D
Massachusetts	12	D	D	D	R	R	D	D	D
Michigan	18	D	R	D	R	R	R	D	D
Minnesota	10	D	R	D	D	D	D	D	D
Mississippi	7	AI	R	D	R	R	R	R	R
Missouri	11	R	R	D	R	R	R	D	D
Montana	3	R	R	R	R	R	R	D	R
Nebraska	5	R	R	R	R	R	R	R	R
Nevada	4	R	R	R	R	R	R	D	D
New Hampshire	4	R	R	R	R	R	R	D	D
New Jersey	15	R	R	R	R	R	R	D	D
New Mexico	5	R	R	R	R	R	R	D	D
New York	33	D	R	D	R	R	D	D	D
North Carolina	14	Rᵃ	R	D	R	R	R	R	R
North Dakota	3	R	R	R	R	R	R	R	R
Ohio	21	R	R	D	R	R	R	D	D
Oklahoma	8	R	R	R	R	R	R	R	R
Oregon	7	R	R	R	R	R	D	D	D
Pennsylvania	23	D	R	D	R	R	R	D	D
Rhode Island	4	D	R	D	D	R	D	D	D
South Carolina	8	R	R	D	R	R	R	R	R
South Dakota	3	R	R	R	R	R	R	R	R
Tennessee	11	R	R	D	R	R	R	D	D
Texas	32	D	R	D	R	R	R	R	R
Utah	5	R	R	R	R	R	R	R	R
Vermont	3	R	R	R	R	R	R	D	D
Virginia	13	R	Rᵃ	R	R	R	R	R	R
Washington	11	D	R	Ra	R	R	D	D	D
West Virginia	5	D	R	D	D	R	D	D	D
Wisconsin	11	R	R	D	R	R	Da	D	D
Wyoming	3	R	R	R	R	R	R	R	R

Source: Presidential Elections, 1789–1996 (Washington, D.C.: Congressional Quarterly, 1997), 84.

Note: AI = American Independent; R = Republican; D = Democratic.

[a] Includes faithless elector who did not support candidate winning popular majority in state.

Table 4-2 Characteristics of Voters in States with Greatest Electoral Votes, 1996

Characteristic	California	New York	Texas
Gender			
Female	52%	54%	52%
Male	48	46	48
Age			
18-29	17	17	17
30-44	31	32	34
45-59	25	27	26
60+	28	24	23
Race			
White	76	80	71
Black	6	9	10
Hispanic	12	7	17
Asian	4	2	1
Other	2	2	1
Religion			
Protestant	35	24	42
Catholic	27	45	25
Other Christian	13	9	21
Jewish	5	10	1
Other/None	20	12	10
Income			
Less than $15,000	10	11	12
$15,000-$29,999	17	20	21
$30,000-$49,999	26	27	26
$50,000-$74,999	23	21	21
More than $75,000	24	21	20
Education			
Did not complete high school	4	6	10
High school graduate	18	21	19
Some college	31	22	32
College graduate	26	29	25
Postgraduate	20	21	14
Party affiliation			
Democrat	42	42	36
Republican	38	29	37
Independent/Other	21	28	27
Ideology			
Conservative	33	27	44
Moderate	45	48	41
Liberal	22	25	15

Source: Voter News Service.

Note: Some columns total less than 100 percent because respondents did not know or refused to answer.

Table 4-3 Popular Vote versus Electoral College Vote, 1968–1996

Election	Candidate	Party	Popular vote	Electoral vote
1968	Richard Nixon	R	31,785,480	301
	Hubert H. Humphrey	D	31,275,166	191
	George C. Wallace	AI	9,906,473	46
1972	Richard Nixon	R	47,169,911	520
	George McGovern	D	29,170,383	17
1976	Jimmy Carter	D	40,830,763	297
	Gerald R. Ford	R	39,147,793	240
1980	Ronald Reagan	R	43,904,153	489
	Jimmy Carter	D	35,483,883	49
	John B. Anderson	I	5,720,060	0
1984	Ronald Reagan	R	54,455,075	525
	Walter F. Mondale	D	37,577,185	13
1988	George Bush	R	48,886,097	426
	Michael S. Dukakis	D	41,809,074	111
1992	Bill Clinton	D	44,909,326	370
	George Bush	R	39,103,882	168
	Ross Perot	I	19,741,657	0
1996	Bill Clinton	D	47,402,357	379
	Bob Dole	R	39,198,755	159
	Ross Perot	RF	8,085,402	0

Source: Presidential Elections, 1789-1996 (Washington, D.C.: Congressional Quarterly, 1997), 68–75, 120–127.

Note: R = Republican; D = Democratic; AI = American Independent; I = Independent; RF = Reform.

Table 4-4 Public Support for the Major Parties, 1952–1996

Year	Identify with a party	Is neutral toward both parties	Is positive toward one party and negative toward the other	Split ticket between president and representative
1952	75%	13%	50%	12%
1956	73	16	40	16
1960	75	17	41	14
1964	77	20	38	15
1968	70	17	38	26
1972	64	30	30	30
1976	63	31	31	25
1980	64	37	27	34
1984	64	36	31	25
1988	63	30	34	25
1992	61	32	34	36
1996	65	30	33	25

Source: SRC/CPS National Election Studies; Calculations by Martin P. Wattenberg.

Table 4-5   Vote for Presidential Candidates by Party Identification, 1968–1996

Election	Candidates	Democrats	Republicans	Independents
1968	Hubert H. Humphrey (D)	74%	9%	31%
	Richard Nixon (R)	12	86	44
	George C. Wallace (AI)	14	5	25
1972	George McGovern (D)	67	5	31
	Richard Nixon (R)	33	95	69
1976	Jimmy Carter (D)	82	9	38
	Gerald R. Ford (R)	18	91	57
	Eugene J. McCarthy (I)	—	—	4
1980	Jimmy Carter (D)	69	8	29
	Ronald Reagan (R)	26	86	55
	John B. Anderson (I)	4	5	14
1984	Walter F. Mondale (D)	79	4	33
	Ronald Reagan (R)	21	96	67
1988	Michael S. Dukakis (D)	85	7	43
	George Bush (R)	15	93	57
1992	Bill Clinton (D)	82	7	39
	George Bush (R)	8	77	30
	Ross Perot (I)	10	16	31
1996	Bill Clinton (D)	90	10	48
	Bob Dole (R)	6	85	33
	Ross Perot (RF)	4	5	19

Source: The Gallup Organization

Note: D = Democratic; R = Republican; AI = American Independent; I = Independent; RF = Reform; — = less than 1 percent. Percentages have been rounded to the nearest whole number.

Table 4-6   Considerations in Casting a Vote, 1996

Option	Voters who said option mattered	Clinton's share of vote among voters choosing option	Dole's share of vote among voters choosing option	Perot's share of vote among voters choosing option
He shares my view of government	20%	41%	46%	10%
He stands up for what he believes in	13	42	40	16
He cares about people like me	9	72	17	9
He is honest and trustworthy	20	8	84	7
He is in touch with the 1990s	10	89	8	4
He has a vision for the future	16	77	13	9

Source: Voter News Service.

Note: The question was, "Which one candidate quality mattered the most in deciding how you voted for president?" Totals do not add to 100 percent because responses of voters who supported other third-party or independent candidates are not reported.

FIGURE 4-1   Poll Standings of the Major Candidates, September–November 1996

Percentage

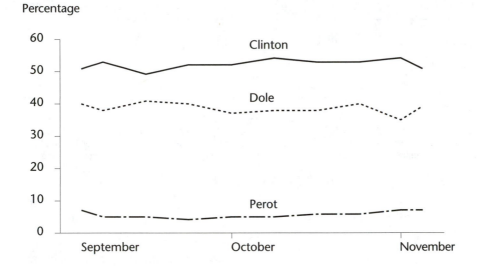

Source: ABC News.

Note: The question was, "The candidates in November's presidential election are Bill Clinton and Al Gore, the Democrats; Bob Dole and Jack Kemp, the Republicans; and Ross Perot and Pat Choate, the Reform Party candidates. Suppose the election were being held today; for whom would you vote?" Before September 15, the question did not contain the names of the vice presidential candidates.

Table 4-7 Characteristics of General Election News, 1988–1996

Coverage	1996	1992	1988
Amount			
Number of stories	483	728	589
Minutes per day	12	25	17
Average soundbite (seconds)	8.2	8.4	9.8
Focus (percentage of stories)			
Horse race	48%	58%	58%
Policy issues	37	32	39
Tone (percentage of good press)			
Democratic nominee	50%	52%	31%
Republican nominee	33	29	38
Independent or Reform Party nominee	32	45	—

Table 4-7 *Continued*

Coverage	1996	1992	1988
Voice (percentage of air time)			
Reporter/anchor	73%	71%	—
Candidate	13	12	—
Other	14	17	—

Source: Center for Media and Public Affairs.

Note: Figures reflect content analysis of all campaign news stories on ABC, CBS, and NBC evening newscasts from September 5 through November 7, 1988; September 7 through November 2, 1992; and September 2 through November 4, 1996. Missing data reflect that no major independent or Reform Party candidate ran in 1988 and that voice of coverage was not calculated for 1988.

Exercises

1. Review the 2000 general election campaign, focusing on unplanned events that affected the outcome of the election. What were these events? How did each candidate deal with them? Which candidate did they help and which candidate did they hurt?

2. Poll your classmates on their general election choice. Ask what they perceive the skills and characteristics of each candidate to be, how their policy positions compare with those of each candidate, and what their party affiliations are.

Review the results, identifying the strongest correlates of support for each candidate. Which factor appears to be most important—perception of candidate skills and characteristics, perception of the match of candidate and respondent positions on issues, or party affiliation?

3. Review several general campaign advertisements. Identify both the stated and unstated assertions of the ad. Are these assertions correct?

4. Write a script for a thirty-second television advertisement for any of the major candidates in the 2000 general election. Identify the particular media markets where the ad would be most appropriate. Explain why.

5. Using information found in Table 4-2, develop a campaign strategy for any major candidate in California, New York, or Texas—the three states with the largest number of electoral votes. The campaign should be tailored to the particular characteristics of voters in the state. Which groups of voters should the campaign emphasize? What issues could be used to mobilize these voters?

6. After completing Exercise 5, develop a national campaign strategy for any major party or independent candidate in the 2000 general election.

First, identify a strategy to achieve a majority of 270 electoral votes. This strategy should include the states and groups of voters that the campaign will focus on and the issues that will be used to mobilize these voters. Second, develop another strategy that assumes the electoral college will be deadlocked and that the selection of the president will be made by the House of Representatives. What states will be targeted and why? What kinds of direct or indirect appeals will be made to members of the House who ultimately will select the president?

7. Review a selection of campaign advertisements by the major candidates to identify the themes of the 2000 campaign. Can the election results be explained by the success, or lack of success, of these themes?

8. After reviewing a selection of news reports on the campaign, categorize them by the orientation of the coverage. What was the focus, tone, and voice of the coverage (see Table 4-7)? If you reviewed both network and local news, how did their coverage compare?

9. Choose a state and analyze the results of the presidential election. How did particular regions of the state or groups within the state vote? Identify issues and candidate positions that may have determined the results.

10. Political scientists have identified "critical elections" as ones in which the landscape of American politics is transformed. A different political party becomes the dominant party when voters in large number change their political affiliations or when new voters enter the political arena. Drastic changes in the composition of the House of Representatives and the Senate often accompany such a shift. Can the 2000 election be considered a critical election? Why or why not?

11. Review the role of third-party or independent candidates in the 2000 election. What role did they play in the campaign and election?

12. Identify new telecommunications technology that was used by candidates during the 2000 general election. Can any candidate or campaign be considered a telecommunications innovator? What was the overall impact of this new technology on the outcome of the election?

13. What was the effect of the Internet on the 2000 election? Before you answer this question, be sure to explain what exact indexes or criteria you are using to answer the question.

14. Review and evaluate the role that the media played in the 2000 general election. What was different compared with past elections? Do you consider these differences to be positive or negative changes? Explain.

Additional Sources

Printed Material and Videos

Berns, Walter, ed. *After the People Vote: A Guide to the Electoral College*. Washington, D.C.: AEI Press, 1992. A concise review of the relevant constitutional provisions and statutes governing the workings of the electoral college. Do you know which states still list electors on their presidential ballot? This volume will tell you.

The Best Spots of 1996. Videos of over 100 of the most notable campaign commercials from the 1996 general election, available from *Campaigns and Elections* magazine in Washington, D.C. An invaluable supplement to studying an increasingly critical aspect of campaigning.

Brown, Robert J. *Manipulating the Ether: The Power of Broadcast Radio in Thirties America*. Jefferson, N.C.: McFarland, 1998. Several chapters review FDR's innovative use of this new medium in his campaigns.

Mondak, Jeffrey J. *Nothing to Read*. Ann Arbor: University of Michigan Press, 1995. How do citizens gain information about candidates and campaigns when the local newspaper is on strike? This volume assesses the impact of the media on voters in this situation.

Patterson, Thomas E. *Out of Order*. New York: Knopf, 1993. What happens when the media attempt to perform critical political functions related to selecting the president? Patterson reviews this development and makes some suggestions as to how we might begin to resolve this dilemma.

Thompson, Kenneth W., ed. *Lessons from Defeated Presidential Candidates*. Lanham, Md.: University Press of America, 1994. This intriguing book is the transcript of presentations and discussion on losing presidential campaigns. These presentations and discussions occurred at a series of forums at the Miller Center of the University of Virginia. The topics range from Charles Evans Hughes's defeat in 1916 to Walter Mondale's loss in 1984.

Wattenberg, Martin P. *The Decline of American Political Parties, 1952–1996*. Cambridge: Harvard University Press, 1998. A systematic and thorough argument that the public increasingly views parties as irrelevant.

Online Data

Center for Media and Public Affairs. This is the site of an organization that analyzes the content and bias of news. The election studies are invaluable for understanding what the public does and does not learn about candidates and campaigns from contemporary news coverage.

> To access: http://www.cmpa.com/

Electoral College Internet Activities and Links. This site of the Department of Government and Economics at Houston Community College Central will provide you with more information about the workings of the electoral college than you ever wanted to know.

> To access:http://ccollege.hccs.cc.tx.us/ instru/govecon/ec.htm

National Election Studies. This site provides access to a voluminous data set on public opinion and electoral behavior developed by the Center for Political Studies at the University of Michigan. Responses to a small portion of the questions are presented in an online guide. For the more adventurous, data sets for 1952–1996 may be downloaded or manipulated. This site is a must for any serious student of elections.

> To access:http://www.umich.edu/~nes/

Project Whistlestop. This site is part of a cooperative project of the Harry S. Truman Library and Museum and other educational institutions to create a digital archive of the Truman years. This part of the project focuses on the 1948 presidential campaign. The information presented is quite detailed and often organized into exercises for students.

> To access:http://www.whistlestop.org/

Yahoo. This is one of the best sites on the Internet for politics. Yahoo's "2000 Presidential Race" is a virtual library of campaign coverage, presenting an incredible array of links. This should be your first online stop for investigating campaign 2000.

> To access:http://headlines.yahoo.com/ Full_Coverage/US/Presidential_ Elections_2000/

Protesters from the National Campaign Finance Reform Coalition wave signs and shout slogans at guests attending a Bush/Quayle fundraiser at the Washington Convention Center. While much has changed since 1992, campaign finance reform remains a hotly debated issue in the 2000 election.

(Source: R. Michael Jenkins, Congressional Quarterly)

Controversies for the Future

One characteristic of American politics is its periodic review of the most fundamental institutions of elected government. This reevaluation, often called "reform," may portray particular institutions as hopelessly flawed, undemocratic, unrepresentative, unaccountable, or inefficient.

Areas of Controversy

The laws, customs, and practices that govern the way Americans elect their chief executive are not exempt from this reevaluation. Numerous controversial aspects of the presidential selection process have come under review. Some parts of the process have changed much and still are under attack. Others have changed little, despite continued and vociferous criticism.

The 1996 presidential election was beset by widespread allegations of illegal campaign finance activity and historically low voter turnout. Although these two facets of the election reflect considerable dissatisfaction with the presidential selection process as it currently operates, a sufficient catalyst for change does not yet exist. The disparate and often contradictory sources of discontent have failed to produce a consensus on what changes should be made in the presidential selection process. Nonetheless, declining support for the major parties, increasing anti-Washington and

anti–central government sentiments, and continuing concern about issueless campaigns that depress participation by citizens have all helped to focus attention on the need for electoral reform.

Proposals for change have focused on the role of government in campaign finance, the influence of the media on campaigns, citizens' access to registration and the vote, candidates' access to the ballot, and the mechanisms that translate voters' preferences into successful candidacies.

Campaign Finance

The 1996 presidential election revealed several areas of concern in campaign finance. Among them were illegal foreign contributions to the Democratic campaign, record expenditures by or on behalf of the presidential nominees, and rapid growth in campaign-related fund raising and spending outside the purview of federal campaign finance laws. The Federal Election Commission investigated spending by both the Democratic and Republican National Committees in support of their presidential candidates. All these developments suggest the demise of the campaign finance regulation system that has been in place since the 1976 presidential election.

In the 1970s, in response to charges that candidates with greater financial resources had unfair advantages and the Watergate revelations of the corrupting influence of money on the policy-making process, Congress moved to regulate money in presidential elections. The 1971 Federal Election Campaign Act was followed by amendments in 1974, 1976, and 1979 and by several Supreme Court decisions that altered some of its provisions.

Under current federal campaign finance law candidates in the presidential primaries receive partial public funding, and candidates in the general election campaign are provided with public grants (approximately $66 million for each major party nominee in 2000). In return for public funds, candidates agree to spending limits during the prenomination period and in the general election campaign. Individuals are permitted to contribute no more than $1,000 to any presidential candidate running in the primary election campaign, and they are prohibited from contributing directly to any presidential candidate in the general election. The law also allots $3 million plus cost-of-living adjustments to each major party to finance its national convention (approximately $13.5 million in 2000). It allows, but limits, national party expenditures on behalf of a candidate (approximately $13 million in 2000). Finally, the Federal Election Commission has the authority to review the eligibility of presidential candidates for public funds, to certify payment of those funds, and to audit all recipients of public funding to make sure that funds were spent in compliance with the law.

The widespread use of loopholes, however, has essentially gutted the Federal Election Campaign Act and its amendments. Most prominently, several kinds of contributions to candidates and expenditures by or on behalf of candidates are not regulated or are regulated by very loose standards. For example, money raised or spent by national political parties for a variety of activities that affect presidential campaigns at the state and local levels is not regulated. Such money, popularly called "soft money," is designed solely to support state and local party activities. In practice, these funds

have been targeted to be spent on activities that benefit presidential candidates. In essence, this has meant unlimited expenditures on activities that are an integral part of presidential campaigns. It also means that unlimited amounts of money, designated for state and local party purposes but with a clear impact on federal elections, may be transferred among state and national party committees. This milewide loophole was in evidence shortly before the 1998 midterm election when the state campaign committee of Texas governor (and prospective presidential candidate) George W. Bush Jr. gave $200,000 to a soft money account of the Republican National Committee.

In addition, political action committees (PACs), which are established specifically to raise and spend money in federal elections, are an available source of funds before and during the presidential campaign. Leadership PACs—committees organized by nationally prominent politicians who are also often prospective presidential candidates—have become a source of organizational resources and funds to support campaign-like activities before a candidate has formally declared for office. By avoiding the expenditure limits of the Federal Election Campaign Act that are triggered once a candidate declares, potential candidates can use these vehicles to pursue effectively what one scholar labels the "shadow campaign." In the current presidential election cycle, candidates have also established state PACs that can raise and spend money in conjunction with federal PACs as part of the precampaign phase.

PACs can serve this purpose because the Federal Election Campaign Act and state campaign finance laws regulate them by standards that are more liberal than those for individuals—or do not regulate them at all. Under federal law, individuals may contribute only $1,000 to a presidential primary contender; PACs may contribute five times that amount. Individuals may contribute no more than a total of $25,000 to candidates in any one calendar year; no aggregate limit has been set on PAC giving. In using this "hard," or regulated, money, a PAC may also spend an unlimited amount in support of or in opposition to a candidate. In federal campaigns, these expenditures on behalf of or against a candidate—called "express advocacy—must be disclosed, raised according to contribution limits, and come from acceptable sources.

PACs are also effective vehicles to support campaigns and candidates because they are allowed to establish soft money accounts. There is no limit to the amount of soft money that may be given to a PAC. And there is no limit to what a PAC may spend or what it may transfer from its own soft money accounts to those of another PAC or committee. As long as a communication from a PAC does not explicitly urge a vote for or against a candidate, soft money may be used—although the candidate may be condemned or praised in conjunction with a particular stand or an issue (this is called "issue advocacy"). Under federal law the source and amount of this kind of expenditure does not have to be disclosed.

As a result of recent court decisions, national party committees now have an equal license to use soft money for issue advertising. Indeed, both Bill Clinton's and Bob Dole's campaigns in 1996 were substantially aided by this kind of unlimited party spending. The focus of the inquiry by the Federal Election Commission was whether, as required by law, this spending was truly independent of the respective presidential campaigns. (For a review of 1996 campaign spending, see Box 5-1.)

The controversy surrounding PACs, soft money, and issue advocacy reflects a broader problem inherent in the Federal Election Campaign Act: inadequately regulated monies fuel the search for additional monies to fund presidential campaigns. Campaign costs have risen rapidly, while the value of the dollar has declined. Yet the limit on individual contributions to campaigns has remained the same. The maximum $1,000 individual contribution has lost more than half its value since the inception of the limit in 1975. Furthermore, state and aggregate limits on campaign spending are increasingly unrealistic, and public funding for presidential campaigns is inadequate and, given projected deficits in the public fund, unreliable. There are now a number of participants, beyond the major party candidates, spending considerable sums to influence voters in presidential campaigns. And an increasing number of self-financed candidates have carte blanche to spend unlimited amounts. In sum, the current state of presidential campaign finance regulation is seriously flawed and is undergoing scrutiny not seen since Watergate, which spawned much of the current law.

Congress, however, has been unable to reach any agreement on solutions. And, despite House and Senate investigations into high-profile campaign finance irregularities in the 1996 election, voters rarely identify campaign finance reform as one of the nation's priorities. In the 105th Congress (1997–1999), a campaign finance reform bill passed in the House, 237–186, but a comparable bill died in the Senate. The bill prohibited national parties and federal candidates from raising or spending soft money, tightened the definition of what was a coordinated expenditure, and required interest groups to pay for issue advocacy with regulated (and thereby limited) "hard" dollars.

In the 106th Congress, advocates of campaign finance reform reintroduced this legislation. The House is scheduled to debate it, along with several others, in September 1999. Passage of this legislation in both legislative bodies, however, will be difficult if not impossible. The majority Republican leadership is either opposed to it or lukewarm. Critics argue that the proposed legislation either violates free speech or does not solve the basic problem of insufficient regulated monies to pay for increasingly expensive campaigns.

In the meantime, public support for Washington-based solutions to campaign finance problems has declined significantly. Campaign finance legislation was originally designed to level the financial playing field with a combination of federal restrictions and monies, but the public's perception of such legislation now is different from what it was in past elections. Indeed, the general perception of independent Ross Perot, whose 1992 presidential campaign was self-financed, or of Republican Steve Forbes, whose 1996 (and 2000 campaign) was also self-financed, is not necessarily that of a "fat cat" buying an election but rather of an individual whose wealth has allowed him to remain free from corrupting federal influence and dollars.

Governor Bush's decision not to accept public financing, and thereby avoid expenditure limits in the pre–general election period in 2000, has yet to produce any apparent negative effect on his campaign, despite the efforts of several of his Republican opponents to make it an issue. Declining public participation in the tax check-off program, which forced Congress in 1993 to raise the check-off amount from one to three dollars, is another sign that the public's conception of campaign finance reform includes a shrinking role for Washington and central government.

The Media's Role

Another source of controversy is the powerful role that the mass media perform in conveying information to the public about the presidential selection process. From evaluating candidates to providing general cues about politics, the media have become important players in presidential campaigns. Their increasingly important role has generally been accepted as a fact of life in American politics. Certain events, however, have triggered criticism and have led concerned citizens and Congress to look for ways to refashion or reform the part played by the media.

In the 1988 and 1992 presidential elections, for example, media-generated controversies that focused on the private side of candidates' lives led to campaigns in which discussions of public policy issues were often eclipsed. After what was generally considered to be poor coverage of policy issues during the 1988 campaign, the media promised to do better in 1992. There were some changes in campaign coverage, such as newspapers' careful and systematic reviews of campaign advertisements (labeled by some as "truth boxes"). However, by the time of the 1992 general election, the number of stories on network evening newscasts that focused on policy issues was even smaller than in 1988, and the average number of seconds in a story in which the candidates spoke for themselves was reduced even further.

In the 1996 election the media avoided the vocal criticism of their coverage that had been common in the previous two elections. The big media story in 1996 was not the change in the orientation of coverage but its overall decline. According to the Center for Media and Public Affairs, network evening coverage of the 1996 election from Labor Day to election day was 44 percent less than in the comparable period in 1992. For the public, however, less was not necessarily bad. In a poll conducted by the *Washington Post,* Harvard University, and the Kaiser Family Foundation, the majority of the respondents said that they felt sufficiently knowledgeable to make an informed choice by election day and that the media had treated the candidates fairly.

Although muted in 1996, complaints about the media's interest in the personal foibles of candidates or in campaign strategies rather than in substantive discussion of policy issues have not disappeared. These complaints are part of a larger critique of the overall role of the American mass media in the political process. Many have argued that the media's changing definition of "news" has led to a precipitous decline in the quality of political debate and discussion that is most starkly exhibited in presidential campaigns. In part, this has resulted from the narrowing of differences between elite newspapers and television network news, on the one hand, and the tabloid and sensationalist press, on the other. An example of this trend was the mainstream media's preoccupation in 1992 with an alleged extramarital affair by Governor Clinton, despite the fact that the allegation was first raised by a tabloid newspaper. The rise of the Internet as a news source has furthered this trend with the explosion of sites proffering stories whose origins are unclear and facts unverified.

Although the decline in the quality of public discourse is related to a number of complex and interrelated changes in American society, the focus of campaign reform efforts to improve it periodically returns to the mass media. Most proposals for improvement focus on ways in which candidates and campaigns can gain substantially unmediated access to the media at reduced cost or no cost. To achieve this goal, some have suggested voluntary compliance by the media; others have suggested federal mandates or incentives to encourage media cooperation.

In the 1996 presidential election, advocates of free time for candidates secured modest cooperation from the networks. CBS, for example, carried four nights of two-and-a-half-minute statements by candidates on the *CBS Evening News*, while NBC aired five evenings of ninety-second statements on *Dateline*. Despite the hopes of advocates that the free spots would essentially be a nightly dialogue between President Clinton and Senator Dole, candidates' messages were often recycled lines from old speeches. The networks and newspapers did little to promote the free-time experiments, and, not surprisingly, most Americans did not watch. In the 1998 state and federal elections, free-time advocates were successful in gaining the cooperation of more than sixty commercial television stations in providing candidates free air time for short unedited statements or mini-debates.

Advocates of government mandates ensuring free time for candidates have also been active. The major campaign finance bills that were blocked in the 105th Congress but reintroduced in the 106th contain free or reduced costs for television time for congressional candidates. In 1997 President Clinton established, by executive order, the Advisory Committee on Public Interest Obligations of Digital Television

Broadcasters and urged it to recommend some form of government mandates for free air time. The committee, however, could not agree on mandates and recommended instead the voluntary participation of television stations in providing forums for five minutes a night in the thirty days preceding the general election. The committee also suggested that free time should be part of campaign finance reform. In 1998, at the urging of both President Clinton and Vice President Gore, the Federal Communications Commission began studying whether free air time should be mandated as part of a broadcaster's public interest obligation.

Another dimension of the free-time controversy is the media's bias against third-party and independent candidates. These candidates receive minimal news coverage and generally are excluded from media-sponsored debates. Their invisibility in the press has a snowball effect by prompting other civic and nonpartisan organizations to exclude third-party and independent candidates from campaign events. In 1996, for example, most networks that voluntarily offered free time to candidates restricted their offers to the major party nominees. Additionally, the sponsor of the 1996 presidential and vice presidential debates, the nonprofit Commission on Presidential Debates, invited only major party nominees. Efforts to combat this bias have proceeded through the courts and in Congress. Currently, several independents or third-party candidates excluded from the 1996 presidential debates are suing in federal court, while at least two bills have been introduced in the 106th Congress establishing new ground rules for presidential debates. Others have urged the Federal Election Commission to develop criteria for the inclusion of candidates in presidential debates.

The media have also been criticized for reporting voting trends or predicting winners on the basis of exit interviews before the polls have closed across the country. In particular, Democrats and Republicans in the western United States have feared that this practice would discourage voters from participating in federal and state elections. Democrats, for example, charged that the networks' early predictions on election night in 1980 that President Jimmy Carter had lost the election to Ronald Reagan kept many western Democrats from voting, thereby damaging the chances of Democratic candidates for the Senate and the House of Representatives. Western Republicans expressed a similar concern in 1996, when they feared that an expected Clinton landslide in the Northeast might prompt the networks to make early predictions of his reelection.

Although these complaints have a partisan tinge to them, a number of studies, according to the nonpartisan Committee for the Study of the American Electorate, show a drop of voting between 0.5 and 3 percent because of network projections of winners. The networks ultimately agreed that, beginning in 1986, they would not predict winners in particular states until the polls had closed. This agreement, however, did not prevent them from declaring a winner in presidential elections in 1988, 1992, and 1996 before polls had closed in some western states. It also did not prevent them from being wrong in their prediction in one Republican presidential primary and in one Senate race on election night in 1996. This controversy took a somewhat new twist in 1996, when *ABC News* mistakenly posted dummy election returns and predictions on its Web site early on election eve. Many in Congress assert that the only real solution is to establish a uniform schedule of voting throughout the nation. Legislation has been introduced in Congress that would require all polls in the United States to close at 11:00 p.m. eastern standard time.

Despite the introduction of numerous pieces of legislation in Congress to deal with these controversies, change in the role of the media in the presidential selection process is unlikely to occur through government regulation. To begin with, the controversy has cooled somewhat because both candidates and campaigns have taken a wait-and-see attitude as both the presidential selection process and the media undergo change. Many candidates now believe that the availability of new media formats and the Internet will bolster substantially their ability to circumvent media bias. This attitude, however, could change rapidly. Governor Bush's early success in cornering campaign contributions and media attention—to the detriment of his Republican competitors—may convince those normally unsympathetic to reform that some regulation of the media may be appropriate. Ultimately, however, the debate over reform of the media hinges to a large degree on a sensitive and difficult question: In a nation with a free press, what degree of government regulation of the mass media is tolerable?

Access to the Ballot: Voters

Who may vote and how qualified voters are screened or identified are questions that have been answered in different ways throughout American history. African Americans, for example, enjoyed suffrage in the period directly after the Civil War. By the turn of the century, however, most had been excluded from the polling booth. This situation changed once again with the civil rights movement in the 1960s. In several midwestern states, noncitizens could vote until the mid-nineteenth century. Women were generally excluded from the franchise until the Nineteenth Amendment to the Constitution gave them the vote in 1920.

In the past several decades, the franchise has been strengthened further among existing voters and has been opened to new groups. Discrimination against African American voters was curbed in 1965 through the Voting Rights Act. In 1971 the Twenty-sixth Amendment extended the vote to citizens who were eighteen years or older. Hispanics and other language minorities were enfranchised in 1975 by amendments to the Voting Rights Act. Additionally, the Equal Access to Voting Rights Act of 1984 made voting more accessible to the infirm and those with disabilities. Individual states also are pursuing arrangements by which voters could cast a ballot before election day or secure an absentee ballot on demand. By 1996 twelve states had instituted early voting, and eighteen states had liberal rules for absentee voting. In 1996 both Oregon and North Dakota held presidential primaries by mail. Beginning in 1999 Oregon planned to conduct all of its federal elections by mail.

Voting was initially an informal and public process. As popular politics developed by the 1830s, parties, candidates, and newspapers began printing marked ballots that voters deposited in the ballot box. Voting was essentially a public declaration of fealty to a party. As friends watched and cheered, the voter raised the ballot high before depositing it, the vote identifiable through the symbol on the ballot or the color of the ballot. Any regulation of voting to ensure that only qualified residents participated was informal or nonexistent.

Registration (and the secret ballot) was a response to what many saw as the excesses of a system that often produced corrupt governments based on the votes of illiterates and immigrants. By the early twentieth century, most states had instituted voter registration, which had the overall effect of substantially reducing voter participation and, in some states, eliminating entire targeted groups, such as African Americans, from the voter rolls.

The past few decades also have witnessed assaults on restrictive registration practices. The Voting Rights Act of 1965 and its amendments outlawed literacy tests as a precondition to voting and prohibited other practices that prevented African Americans and Hispanics from registering to vote. In 1993 Congress passed the National Voter Registration Act (colloquially known as the "motor voter act"), which made registration easier. Under the new law, states are required to allow residents to register by mail or when they apply for a driver's license. Registration forms must be available at agencies that provide public assistance. Some states have recently moved on their own, without congressional prodding, to ease registration requirements. For the 1996 election six states permitted registration on election day.

Despite the removal of barriers to voter participation, turnout in federal elections has continued to decline (see Figure 5-1). Indeed, at a time when registration and voting are the least restrictive since the implementation of the secret ballot, voting turnout in the 1996 presidential election was the lowest since 1924. It was also the largest single decline from one presidential election to another since 1920. In states with the most liberal registration and voting practices, these arrangements seemed to make little difference. For example, in states that allow registration on election day, voting turnout declined by more than 8 percent from 1992 to 1996, while turnout declined 6 percent on average in other states. In states with liberal absentee voting, voting turnout declined by about 6 percent from 1992 to 1996, as it also did on average in other states.

Although a long and vibrant tradition of American electoral reform has asserted that millions more Americans would come to the polls if registration and voting were made easier, this is clearly no longer the case. What is currently lacking for many Americans is a sense of civic engagement—a notion that politics and political participation are relevant to their lives and can make a difference. Without this political perspective, further liberalization of voting and registration may not matter. Congressional efforts to connect more Americans to the political process have shifted somewhat from attempts to mandate further liberalization of voting and registration procedures, which conservatives and many states oppose, to efforts to connect more Americans with the ballot box through support of emerging new communications technologies, such as the Internet. In particular, many see the current role of government as ensuring that this new technology quickly becomes available and accessible to virtually all Americans. However, innovations made possible by the Internet, such as online registration or voting, also may not make a difference unless this technology helps to re-create citizens' interest in politics. As the Committee for the Study of the American Electorate stressed in its review of registration and voting in the 1996 presidential election, "the problem we have is not procedural but motivational."

Access to the Ballot: Candidates

American electoral politics is characterized by ballot laws that favor well-funded, prominent candidates from the two major parties. At the same time, these laws impose costly restrictions on less well known and underfunded major party candidates and independent or third-party candidates.

The Republican and Democratic Parties use a variety of requirements to discriminate against less-known, underfunded, and often controversial candidates. State parties may require filing fees or petitions with signatures of registered party members. In some states, candidates obtain access to the primary ballot only if they "are discussed by the media." In other states, party officials decide who can be on the ballot. Often these restrictions are so onerous that even nationally prominent (and respected) candidates are excluded. In 1996, for example, New York Republican Party rules required a candidate to petition separately for a spot on the presidential primary ballot in each of New York's thirty-one congressional districts. In each district the candidate had to obtain 1,250 signatures or 5 percent of all registered Republicans. Republican Steve Forbes spent $1 million qualifying for his party's presidential primary ballot in New York. Although Forbes and other Republicans sued in federal court, only Bob Dole, the front-runner, who was supported by most of New York's Republican establishment, and Forbes secured a spot on the ballot in all of the state's congressional districts.

Declining support for the two major parties and a growing number of successful minor party or independent candidates have put pressure on laws and regulations that regulate third-party and independent access to the ballot. Indeed, as a result of the 1996 election returns, thirty-nine states had at least one party guaranteed a ballot position in addition to the Democratic and Republican Parties. In 1992 only four states admitted third-party candidates to their primaries, while in 1996 third-party candidates participated in ten state-run primaries and qualified but declined to participate in another six.

Access to the ballot for independents and third parties has improved nationwide in the past decade, but it still remains difficult and costly in many states. In 1996, according to the Brennan Center for Justice at New York University's law school, independents running for president must gather twenty times as many signatures as prominent candidates from the Democratic or Republican Parties. Third parties must gather at least nine times as many signatures as any major party candidates. Furthermore, major party candidates often are provided with waivers or shortcuts to the ballot. In twenty-three states, waivers were not possible for independent candidates and rarely were available for third-party candidates. Eight states allowed a Democratic or Republican candidate to pay his or her way out of ballot petition requirements. Only three states provided this opportunity for independent candidates. Although some liberalization of ballot access requirements has occurred since the 1996 election, Richard Winger of *Ballot Access News* estimates that a prospective non–major party presidential candidate for 2000 would still need approximately 700,000 signatures to gain a spot on the general election ballot in all fifty states and the District of Columbia. Current estimates are that a third party would have to gather over 3,500,000 signatures to run a slate of candidates in every federal and statewide election in 2000.

Although Congress has held hearings on legislation to make it easier for independent and third-party candidates for federal office to get on the ballot, and ballot access legislation has been introduced in the past several Congresses, opposition to imposing additional ballot requirements on the states has slowed such efforts at the federal level. In contrast, activity at the state level has been intense. By mid-1999 bills that would change the existing ballot requirements for independent or third-party candidates were pending in more than thirty state legislatures. Ballot access has also been pursued vigorously in the state and federal courts. For example, on March 31, 1999, a U.S. district court struck down Arizona's petition process for independents. The law required that independents collect the signatures of 3 percent of all registered independents in the state and submit them by June 27 of election year, The plaintiffs, Green Party activists, successfully argued that it was difficult, if not impossible, to comply with this requirement since independents made up only 14 percent of all registered voters in Arizona. Indeed, no independent candidate for statewide office had ever been able to meet this requirement.

Translating Votes into Victories

Also at issue is the formal process through which citizens' preferences are translated into winning and losing candidates. Preferences for major party candidates may be translated directly into votes for presidential nominees at national party conventions through primaries or caucuses or indirectly through the appointment of party officials or notables as delegates. Supporters of independent or third-party candidates may also hold nominating conventions and use primaries to select participants in these conventions, although in most cases they secure nomination through a state-by-state ballot petition process.

Defenders of the current nomination process argue that it provides an effective means of winnowing the field of candidates while maintaining broad-based national parties that are necessary to govern the nation. Critics assert that the entire process should be fundamentally altered or abolished because most citizens do not participate, those who do participate are not necessarily representative of their party, and the system ultimately produces general election choices among equally flawed candidates (see Table 5-1). Additionally, they argue, contemporary nomination procedures maintain an enfeebled two-party system while making it difficult for other parties or independents to organize and field candidates in November.

The 1996 presidential election and the 1998 congressional elections produced further changes in the nomination process and threaten even more. The 8 percent national vote secured by Ross Perot in 1996 bolstered Reform Party access to primary and general election ballots. The Libertarian Party vote in the 1998 congressional elections, the most for any third party since 1948, qualified that party for the ballot in numerous states. As a result, by July 1999 the Reform Party candidate for the 2000 presidential race was already assured of a spot on twenty-one state ballots, while the Libertarian Party candidate for president had already qualified for thirty state ballots. Perot's candidacy in 1996 also ensured that the Reform Party would have partial public funding in the 2000 general election for president, thereby increasing the likelihood of competition for the Reform Party nomination and a national campaign in the general election.

The 2000 election promises additional changes in the rules and procedures of presidential nomination. Accelerated front loading of delegate selection for the major party conventions has, in effect, brought the nation to the brink of a national primary. Additional gains by independents or third-party candidates will further open the nomination process to their participation. But what ultimately will guide this change is voters' satisfaction with the choices presented in November. A significant level of dissatisfaction with the candidates would focus further attention on the nomination system that produced them.

The fact that presidents are not elected by popular votes but by winning a majority in the electoral college is generally of little consequence, but reform of this aspect of the presidential selection process receives periodic support. The electoral college usually reaffirms the popular verdict on the candidates. When the electoral college has overruled this verdict or narrowly avoided altering it, however, talk of reform moves to center stage. Critics have argued that the electoral college is an archaic remnant of American politics and that popular vote pluralities or majorities should suffice to elect presidents. In 1979 a majority of the Senate voted for a constitutional amendment abolishing the electoral college and establishing direct popular election of the president. The amendment, however, fell short of the required two-thirds vote.

In the elections of 1960, 1968, and 1976 shifts of relatively few popular votes would have left no candidate with an electoral vote majority or would have provided an electoral vote majority to the candidate who had not received the most popular votes (see Table 5-2). With support declining for the two major parties, the possibilities for no clear majority increase greatly. Indeed, during part of the 1992 campaign there was speculation that no presidential candidate would receive a majority in the electoral college and that selecting a president would fall to Congress.

As with many other electoral rules and procedures that may need fixing, Congress is either unable to reach consensus on what to do or is reluctant to impose change on the states. This indecision essentially means that most recent activity related to reform of the electoral college has occurred at the state level. In 1991 Nebraska became the first state in two decades to alter the customary winner-take-all allocation of its electoral votes. New York is debating a similar move.

A Tricky Business

The laws, customs, and practices of presidential politics are not set in stone. Indeed, most of them have undergone considerable change and continue to be scrutinized by the public with a critical eye. When some practice becomes intolerable, changes are proposed, debated, and often implemented.

Electoral reform is a tricky business, however. First, the decentralized nature of American politics invites a variety of players to participate. National parties, state parties, state courts, state legislatures, the Supreme Court, Congress, and the Federal Election Commission, to name but a few, all share responsibility for shaping election laws. As a result, uniform and consistent policy making is rare. Congress, for example, may reject the notion of altering or abolishing the electoral college, but individual states may move to change the allocation schemes of their electoral votes.

Second, all changes in electoral laws have consequences. Many are expected, if not targeted, while others are unforeseen. For example, modifications in the early 1970s in the Democratic rules for selecting delegates to the national convention opened the presidential selection process to groups that had been excluded. However, the changes also drastically reduced representation of elected officials. As a result, the party nominated a presidential candidate without the direct involvement of its congressional delegation—those individuals whom a president would most need to formulate and implement a legislative program. The increased front loading of delegate selection for the major party nominating conventions could have the intended effect of reducing the disproportionate influence of small groups of voters in states such as Iowa and New Hampshire. But it also could have many unforeseen and problematic consequences. By drastically compacting the formal race for the nomination to February and March, candidates have less time to reveal themselves to the American people, raising the possibility that nominees will have been scrutinized only by small numbers of party regulars, not the general public.

Additionally, the brevity of the delegation selection period means that candidates do not have time to solicit new donors on the basis of primary or caucus victories. In this regard, candidates must start raising money years in advance to make sure they have the resources to carry them through the abbreviated period of delegate selection. This, in turn, inserts further biases in favor of nationally known or wealthy candidates who have the means to self-finance a campaign.

Increased front loading, however, could produce another scenario. No amount of money or resources could end up being enough to run simultaneously a dozen primary or caucus campaigns, including several in the nation's largest and most expensive media markets. The result would be candidates focusing only on particular states where they could win or at least secure some delegates through district or proportional allocation schemes. Ultimately, no one candidate would emerge with a majority, ironically producing the first brokered nominating convention in almost a half-century.

Finally, election reform has become increasingly politicized. Although reform of any nature is never devoid of politics, proposed changes in election rules and practices now are an integral part of both presidential campaign strategies and the competition between the two national parties. President Clinton warned that the Democrats should not "unilaterally disarm"

in the name of campaign finance reform. Each party has had its own stance on national registration requirements that unabashedly serves its own interest. Candidates consciously seek to manipulate primary and caucus schedules and the rules for allocation of convention delegates in their favor. Most problematic is the proliferation of election rules and practices that serve candidate and partisan ends at the expense of broader principles that may better serve all citizens and the democracy.

Any changes that are proposed or made in election rules will not be the last. No decade has passed without discussion of proposed changes in the presidential selection process. In some ways, the laws, customs, and practices of this process are a natural focus for the struggle over valued resources in American society because they govern the election of the individual most responsible for the distribution of these resources. In this respect, good citizenship and effective politics share at least one requirement—understanding the rules of the presidential selection process.

Box 5-1 Costs of Electing a President, 1996 (in millions of dollars)

Type of expense	Cost
Prenomination	
Spending by major party candidates	$228.6
RNC spending on Dole nomination campaign	14.0
DNC spending on Clinton nomination campaign	17.0
Spending by minor party candidates	11.7
Independent expenditures	0.7
Communication costs	1.1
Compliance costs	10.0
Subtotal	$282.5
Conventions (including host cities and committees)	
Republicans	$31.0
Democrats	34.0
Subtotal	$65.0
General election	
Spending by major party candidates	$125.2[a]
Parties' coordinated expenditures	18.4[b]
Compliance	13.6
Nonparty organizations[c]	25.0
Spending by minor parties	27.6
Independent expenditures	0.7
Labor, corporate, association spending	20.0
Parties' soft money, issue advertising[d]	68.0
Communication costs	1.6
Subtotal	$300.1
Miscellaneous expenses[e]	$52.4
Total	$700.0

Sources: Citizens' Research Foundation; Herbert E. Alexander, "Spending in the 1996 Elections," in *Financing the 1996 Election,* ed. John Green (Armonk, N.Y.: M. E. Sharpe, 1999).

[a] Includes $61.8 million in public funds spent by each major party ticket.

[b] Includes $11.7 million in "hard money" coordinated expenditures by the RNC and $6.7 million by the DNC.

[c] Includes a reasonable portion of funds spent by nonpartisan organizations to conduct voter registration and get-out-the-vote drives that benefited presidential candidates.

[d] Includes "soft money" expenditures related to the presidential campaigns by the DNC and the RNC.

[e] Miscellaneous out-of-pocket expenditures at all levels.

FIGURE 5-1   Presidential Year Registration and Voting, 1960–1996

Percentage

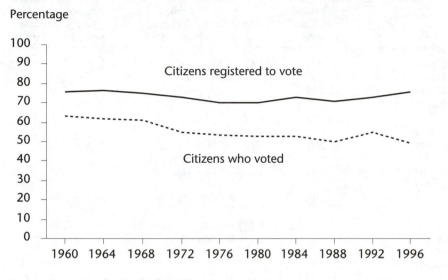

Source: Committee for the Study of the American Electorate.

Note: Registration and voting as a percentage of the voting age population.

Table 5-1   Turnout in Major Party Primaries, 1972–1996

Year	Democratic primaries	Republican primaries
1972	19.7%	8.1%
1976	17.5	11.1
1980	14.8	11.0
1984	16.1	6.6
1988	15.9	8.6
1992	13.2	8.2
1996	8.1	8.6

Source: Committee for the Study of the American Electorate.

Table 5-2　Close Calls in the Electoral College, 1960, 1968, 1976

Election	Party	Electoral college vote	Change in popular vote that would have caused a deadlock	Deadlocked electoral college vote that would have resulted
1960	Democratic (elected)	303	4,430 in Illinois and 4,992 in Missouri	263
	Republican (defeated)	219		259
	Independent (defeated)	15		15
1968	Republican (elected)	301	30,631 in New Jersey, 10,245 in Missouri, and	268
	Democratic (defeated)	191	12,158 in New Hampshire	224
	American Independent (defeated)	46		46
1976	Democratic (elected)	297	6,383 in Delaware and 5,559 in Ohio	269
	Republican (defeated)	240		268
	Republican (defeated)	1[a]		1

Source: Presidential Elections, 1789–1996 (Washington, D.C.: Congressional Quarterly, 1997).

[a] One Republican elector from the state of Washington voted for former president Ronald Reagan.

Table 5-3　Voting-Age Population Registered and Voting, by State, 1996

State	Voting-age population		State	Voting-age population	
	Registered	Voted		Registered	Voted
Alabama	76.8%	47.7	Maryland	67.9	46.7
Alaska	97.6	56.9	Massachusetts	74.8	55.3
Arizona	72.6	45.4	Michigan	94.7	54.5
Arkansas	75.1	47.5	Minnesota	80.0	64.3
California	67.7	43.3	Mississippi	88.3	45.6
Colorado	80.4	53.1	Missouri	83.9	54.2
Connecticut	80.0	56.4	Montana	91.3	63.0
Delaware	76.7	49.6	Nebraska	84.0	56.1
District of Columbia	83.1	42.7	Nevada	66.0	39.4
Florida	73.2	48.0	New Hampshire	82.9	58.0
Georgia	70.1	42.6	New Jersey	72.0	51.2
Hawaii	61.8	40.8	New Mexico	69.2	46.0
Idaho	82.9	58.2	New York	74.8	46.5
Illinois	76.0	49.2	North Carolina	78.5	45.8
Indiana	79.7	48.9	North Dakota	[b]	56.3
Iowa	83.1	57.7	Ohio	82.3	54.3
Kansas	75.7	56.6	Oklahoma	81.8	49.9
Kentucky	82.0	47.5	Oregon	81.9	57.5
Louisiana	81.0	56.9	Pennsylvania	73.9	49.0
Maine	106.6 [a]	64.5	Rhode Island	80.4	52.0

Table 5-3 *Continued*

State	Voting-age population registered	voted	State	Voting-age population registered	voted
South Carolina	65.4	41.5	Virginia	65.3	47.5
South Dakota	89.9	61.1	Washington	74.7	54.7
Tennessee	77.0	47.1	West Virginia	68.7	45.0
Texas	77.2	41.2	Wisconsin	c	57.4
Utah	79.4	50.3	Wyoming	68.4	60.1
Vermont	87.4	58.6			

Source: Committee for the Study of the American Electorate.

[a] Registration figures for Maine reflect more voters than the total state voting-age population.

[b] No registration.

[c] No statewide registration.

Exercises

1. Review the registration laws and the voter turnout in the 2000 presidential election in your state and locality. What effect did these laws have on voter participation? Should these laws be changed? If so, how?

2. The National Voter Registration Act of 1993 helped to raise the national registration rate to an all-time high (see Figure 5-1). Voting turnout in the 1996 presidential election, however, plummeted to a sixty-year low. Can this seeming contradiction be explained by the characteristics of new registrants, particularly those registered through the National Voter Registration Act? Discuss.

3. Using data in Table 5-3, identify two states with disparate registration rates. What might explain these differences?

4. Select any subgroup in the American population (women, African Americans, or Hispanics, for example) and trace changes in registration and suffrage requirements that have affected their political participation throughout U.S. history.

5. Organize a debate with one side arguing that voting is a right and the other arguing that voting is a privilege. As part of the debate, iden-

tify and support registration procedures that correspond with each side's conception of voting.

6. Identify the laws in your state that govern access to the November ballot for third-party or independent presidential candidates. Are these laws appropriate or unfair? Explain.

7. As discussed in this chapter and in Chapter 2, there are many loopholes in the federal campaign finance law that allow candidates to raise and spend unlimited amounts of money. One of the goals of the law was to level the presidential campaign playing field. What should be done to accomplish this goal? Explain.

8. Conduct a class election in three stages, with one-third of the class voting at fifteen-minute intervals. While the first and second groups vote, reporters from the class should interview those who are voting and at the conclusion of the round of voting announce the results to the class. After the election is completed, students who voted in the second and third groups should discuss whether the publicized results of the interviews affected their preference or their desire to vote. What does your discussion suggest about the media's current practice of declaring a winner of the presidential race before all polls have closed?

9. Identify an event that influenced the outcome of either the campaign for nomination or the general election campaign. What was the role of the media in that event? Did the media merely convey information to the public, or did they create or fundamentally shape public opinion related to the event?

10. What is the best way to nominate presidential candidates? Why?

11. Several states are debating whether they should move from a winner-take-all allocation of electoral votes to a district plan in which candidates receive one electoral vote for each congressional district won and two electoral votes for winning the statewide popular vote. Discuss the merits of this plan and its potential effect on presidential campaigns.

12. Debate the pros and cons of the electoral college.

13. Identify one law, custom, or practice related to the presidential election process and review potential catalysts that might prompt its alteration or abolition. For example, a deadlocked electoral college might prompt a public outcry for change in this institution.

14. Review the effect of the much accelerated ("front-loaded") selection of delegates for the major party nominations. Did this change produce expected or unexpected consequences for the presidential selection process?

Additional Sources

Printed Material and Videos

Corrado, Anthony, et al. *Campaign Finance Reform: A Sourcebook.* Washington, D.C.: Brookings Institution, 1997. A great source on the current controversies surrounding campaign finance. This volume includes commentary by notable scholars and primary documents that relate to money in politics.

Rash, Wayne, Jr. *Politics on the Nets.* New York: W. H. Freeman, 1997. One of the first and still perhaps best books on what the Internet is doing to the practice of politics.

Rosen, Jay, and Paul Taylor. *The New News v. the Old News: The Press and Politics in the 1990s.* New York: Twentieth Century Fund, 1992. This book contains two essays that describe the changing nature of the mass media in politics and the potential positive roles the media can perform in the context of rapid and dramatic change.

Rosenkranz, E. Joshua. *Voter Choice '96: A Fifty-State Report Card on the Presidential Elections.* New York: Brennan Center for Justice, 1996. This comprehensive report on state ballot access laws rates each state. According to the report, only Colorado gets an A+.

Schudson, Michael. *The Good Citizen.* New York: Free Press, 1998. Does low voter turnout mean that politics is dead? Not so, according to this author. This intriguing book reviews, with an insightful eye, how Americans historically have participated in politics.

TV Coverage of Candidates Personal Lives. A video, available from C-SPAN Archives, of prominent journalists discussing the appropriate ethical boundaries of campaign reporting.

Online Data

Alliance for Better Campaigns. This is the site of an organization that "seek(s) campaigns in which the most useful information reaches the most citizens in the most engaging way." One part of this approach is to provide more unmediated access through the media for candidates. The site also includes a variety of information related to general campaign reform efforts, especially as they relate to the media.

To access: http://www.bettercampaigns. org

Annenberg Public Policy Center of the University of Pennsylvania. The "Media and the Dialogue of Democracy" section of this site (via "Areas of Research" is full of studies on the quality of discourse in recent campaigns and the role of the media in that discourse.

    To access: http://www.appcpenn.org/

Committee for the Study of the American Electorate. This is the site of the premier organization that collects and analyzes data on registration and voting. The organization has recently begun to focus on campaign finance reform.

    To access: http://tap.epn.org/csae/ index.html

EC WebZine. This site, which is devoted to defending the electoral college, provides great links and interesting commentary. According to the introductory page, "It's time to stand up for the Electoral College, because, frankly, it's under attack."

    To access: http://www.avagara.com/ politics/ec_zine/

Yahoo. The "News: Campaign Finance Reform" section of this site will inform you of everything that is occurring on the campaign finance front.

    To access: http://headlines.yahoo.com/ Full_Coverage/US/Campaign_Finance/

(Source: R. Michael Jenkins, Congressional Quarterly)

Candidate Profiles

This section includes brief profiles of eighteen declared or potential candidates for the 2000 presidential election. Fourteen are Democratic or Republican candidates who had declared by September 1, 1999. Two of these have already dropped out, while a third has left the Republican Party to pursue a presidential bid as an independent or a member of a third party. In some cases, candidates announced exploratory committees with the goal of investigating a possible bid for the presidency. Under federal campaign finance law, however, there is no distinction between an exploratory committee and an official committee established in conjunction with a firm declaration of candidacy. Such distinctions are made by candidates because they provide additional opportunities for media exposure.

All of these individuals are listed here, including the two who dropped out, because any of them may play a role in the presidential sweepstakes in the coming months. Some may turn up in important government positions in the administration of the next president. Four profiles are of third-party candidates who have not yet declared but who promise to play a significant role in their parties' nomination process. Potential nominees of the Reform, Green, and Libertarian Parties are included. These parties received more than 95 percent of the third-party or independent vote for president in 1996.

Each profile contains a general summary of the career of the candidate or potential candidate and a list of Internet sites that provide additional information. The sites listed are suitable for new students of presidential politics who merely want a bit more information about a candidate or for scholars who, for example, may want in-depth campaign finance data. In most cases, the URL links directly to the relevant data, bypassing introductory Web page material. When the link is confusing or unclear—seemingly not relating to the particular candidate—readers should consult the summary section of the profile; it often provides sufficient background to direct the search.

In several profiles, Internet categories remain blank because appropriate sites did not exist as of September 1, 1999. Readers may write in sites in these categories and other categories as they appear and cross out defunct sites as they disappear. In cases where a candidate has withdrawn, some sites may be abandoned. Many, however, will be maintained or linked to updated sites as the campaign progresses. In this regard, this section of the book can serve as a handy campaign Internet guide throughout the presidential selection process.

Lamar Alexander

Alexander, who served as governor of Tennessee (1979–1987), is also a former president of the University of Tennessee. He was appointed secretary of education by President George Bush and made an unsuccessful bid for the Republican nomination for president in 1996. He is affiliated with a leadership PAC, Campaign for a New American Century, and state PACs by the same name in New Hampshire, Tennessee, and Virginia. Additional state PACs include We the Parents, in Tennessee and Virginia. Alexander announced a second candidacy for the Republican nomination for president on March 9, 1999. He dropped out of the race on August 16, 1999, after the Iowa straw poll.

Websites

Official Campaign Headquarters:
Lamar Alexander for President
http://www.lamaralexander.org/

Campaign Finance Data:
Center for Responsive Politics
http://www.opensecrets.org/2000elect/index/
P60003225.htm

Supporters: —

Dirty Laundry:
Lamar Alexander Skeleton Closet
http://www.realchange.org/alexandr.htm

Parodies:
The Daily Muse
http://www.cais.net/aschnedr//lamar.htm

Affiliated Organizations:
We the Parents (VA)
http://www.wetheparents.com/

PAC Finance Data:
Center for Responsive Politics
http://www.opensecrets.org/pacs/
pacgot/00281923.htm

http://www.opensecrets.org/pacs/vadata.htm

FECInfo
http://www.tray.com/cgi-win/_pacwhere.exe?
C00281923

State of New Hampshire
http://www.state.nh.us/sos/filings/

Knox News
http://cfapps.knoxnews.com/state1996/
paclistdetail.cfm?ID=129

Gary Bauer

Bauer is a former domestic policy adviser to President Ronald Reagan. His federal PAC, Campaign for Working Families, played an active role in the 1998 election cycle. Bauer has taken leave from his position as president of the nonprofit Family Research Council to run for the Republican nomination for president. He announced his candidacy on April 21, 1999.

Websites

Official Campaign Headquarters:
Bauer for President 2000
http://www.bauer2k.com/

Campaign Finance Data:
Center for Responsive Politics
http://www.opensecrets.org/2000elect/index/
P00003491.htm

Supporters: —

Dirty Laundry: —

Parodies: —

Affiliated Organizations:
Family Research Council
http://www.frc.org/

Campaign for Working Families
http://www.campaignforfamilies.org/

PAC Finance Data:
Center for Responsive Politics
http://www.opensecrets.org/pacs/pacgot/
00325076.htm

http://www.opensecrets.org/pacs/vadata.htm

FECInfo
http://www.tray.com/cgi-win/_pacwhere.exe?
C00325076

State of New Hampshire
http://www.state.nh.us/sos/filings/

William W. "Bill" Bradley

Bradley represented New Jersey in the U.S. Senate from 1978 through 1996. Before his career in the Senate, he played professional basketball for the New York Knicks. In 1996 he converted his campaign committee into a leadership PAC, Time Future. He is also affiliated with an additional federal PAC, Participation 2000, and a state PAC in New Hampshire, also named Time Future. Bradley is a former chairman of the National Civic League. He declared his candidacy for the Democratic nomination for president on January 8, 1999.

Websites

Official Campaign Headquarters:
Bill Bradley for President
http://www.billbradley.com/

Campaign Finance Data:
Center for Responsive Politics
http://www.opensecrets.org/2000elect/index/P80000516.htm

Supporters:
Bill Bradley for President 2000
http://www.killyourtv.com/billbradley/

Netizens for Bradley
http://www.netizensforbradley.org/

Dirty Laundry:
Bill Bradley Skeleton Closet
http://www.realchange.org/bradley.htm

Parodies: —

Affiliated Organizations:
National Civic League
http://www.ncl.org/ncl/index.htm

PAC Finance Data:
Center for Responsive Politics
http://www.opensecrets.org/pacs/pacgot/00270736.htm

FECInfo
http://www.tray.com/cgi-win/_pacwhere.exe?C00270736

State of New Hampshire
http://www.state.nh.us/sos/filings/

Harry Browne

Browne is an investment adviser, author of nine books, a newsletter writer, radio personality, and public speaker. In 1996 he was the Libertarian Party candidate for president, receiving almost 500,000 votes nationwide. Browne announced the formation of an exploratory committee to consider a bid for the Libertarian Party nomination for president in early 1997.

Websites

Official Campaign Headquarters:
M2K: Momentum 2000 A Project of the Harry Browne 2000 Presidential Exploratory Committee
http://www.harrybrowne2000.org/

Campaign Finance Data: —

Supporters: —

Dirty Laundry:
Harry Browne Skeleton Closet
http://www.realchange.org/browne.htm

Parodies: —

Affiliated Organizations:
Libertarian Party
http://www.lp.org

PAC Finance Data: —

Patrick J. Buchanan

Buchanan served as executive assistant to President Richard Nixon and as director of communications for President Ronald Reagan. He has held numerous positions in print, radio, and television journalism. He is also affiliated with a leadership PAC, America First, and a nonprofit organization, American Cause. Buchanan took a leave of absence from his television show Crossfire and declared his candidacy for the Republican nomination for president on March 2, 1999. There is speculation that he may seek the Reform Party nomination for president.

Websites

Official Campaign Headquarters:
Buchanan 2000
http://www.gopatgo2000.org/

Campaign Finance Data:
Center for Responsive Politics
http://www.opensecrets.org/2000elect/index/P80000805.htm

Supporters:
Pat Buchanan for President in 2000 Link
http://www.iac.net/~davcam/pat.html

Dirty Laundry:
>   Pat Buchanan Skeleton Closet
>   http://www.realchange.org/buchanan.htm

Parodies:
>   Help Wanted—Join the Buchanan Brigade
>   http://www.tiac.net/users/geof/pat.html

Affiliated Organizations:
>   The American Cause
>   http://www.theamericancause.org/

PAC Finance Data:
>   Center for Responsive Politics
>   http://www.opensecrets.org/pacs/
>   pacgot/00254540.htm
>
>   FECInfo
>   http://www.tray.com/cgi-win/_pacwhere.exe?
>   C00254540

George W. Bush Jr.

Bush is the son of former president George Bush. He ran unsuccessfully for Congress in 1978 and was the managing general partner of the Texas Rangers professional baseball team from 1989 through 1994. In 1994 he was elected governor of Texas and reelected in 1998. Bush announced the formation of an exploratory committee to gauge support for a Republican presidential bid on March 8, 1999.

Websites

Official Campaign Headquarters:
>   George W. Bush Presidential Exploratory
>   Committee
>   http://www.georgebush.com/

Campaign Finance Data:
>   Center for Responsive Politics
>   http://www.opensecrets.org/2000elect/index/
>   P00003335.htm
>
>   Texas Ethics Commission
>   http://www.ethics.state.tx.us

Supporters:
>   B2K: The Bush 2000 Network
>   http://www.sas.upenn.edu/~pruffini/
>   bush2000.htm
>
>   Bush Watch
>   http://www.geocities.com/CapitolHill/3750/
>   bush.htm

Dirty Laundry:
>   George W. Bush, Jr. Skeleton Closet
>   http://www.realchange.org/bushjr.htm

Parodies:
>   GWBush.com Presidential Committee
>   http://www.gwbush.com/

Affiliated Organizations:
>   Office of the Texas Governor
>   http://www.governor.state.tx.us/

PAC Finance Data: —

Elizabeth Dole

Dole was secretary of transportation for President Ronald Reagan and secretary of labor for President George Bush. She also served as president of the American Red Cross. Dole announced the formation of an exploratory committee to consider a bid for the Republican nomination for president on March 10, 1999.

Websites

Official Campaign Headquarters:
>   Elizabeth Dole for President Exploratory
>   Committee
>   http://www.edole2000.org/

Campaign Finance Data:
>   Center for Responsive Politics
>   http://www.opensecrets.org/2000elect/index/
>   P00003319.htm

Supporters:
>   President Elizabeth Dole
>   http://elizabethdole.faithweb.com
>
>   National Coalition of Students for Elizabeth
>   Dole
>   http://www.students4dole.com/
>
>   Elizabeth Dole Grassroots
>   http://www2.gdi.net/~paper/dole.htm

Dirty Laundry:
>   Elizabeth Dole Skeleton Closet
>   http://www.realchange.org/dole.htm

Parodies: —

Affiliated Organizations: —

PAC Finance Data: —

Malcolm S. "Steve" Forbes Jr.

Steve Forbes, president of Forbes, Inc., inherited his wealth from the Forbes publishing empire. He ran a largely self-financed and unsuccessful campaign for the Republican nomination for president in 1996. Forbes is affiliated with a private nonprofit organization, Americans for Hope, Growth, and Opportunity, and an Iowa-based organization by the same name. He has also established a leadership PAC—Americans for Hope, Growth, and Opportunity—and a state PAC in New Hampshire by the same name. He declared for the Republican nomination for president on March 16, 1999.

Websites

Official Campaign Headquarters:
Steve Forbes 2000
http://www.forbes2000.com/

Campaign Finance Data:
Center for Responsive Politics
http://www.opensecrets.org/2000elect/index/P60003852.htm

Supporters: —

Dirty Laundry:
Steve Forbes Skeleton Closet
http://www.realchange.org/forbes.htm

Parodies:
Steve Forbes: The Golden Platform
http://www.cais.net/aschnedr//forbes.htm

Affiliated Organizations:
Americans for Hope, Growth & Opportunity
http://www.ahgo.org

Americans for Hope, Growth & Opportunity (Iowa)
http://ahgoiowa.com/

PAC Finance Data:
Center for Responsive Politics
http://www.opensecrets.org/pacs/pacgot/00329888.htm

FECInfo
http://www.tray.com/cgi-win/_pacwhere.exe?C00329888

State of New Hampshire
http://www.state.nh.us/sos/filings/

Albert Gore Jr.

Gore served in Congress from 1976 through 1984 as a representative from Tennessee. In 1984 he was elected to the U.S. Senate from Tennessee and reelected in 1990. Gore was an unsuccessful candidate for the Democratic nomination for president in 1988. He was elected vice president in 1992 and reelected in 1996. He is associated with a leadership PAC, Leadership 98. Gore announced his candidacy for the Democratic nomination for president on June 16, 1999.

Websites

Official Campaign Headquarters:
Gore 2000
http://www.algore2000.com/

Campaign Finance Data:
Center for Responsive Politics
http://www.opensecrets.org/2000elect/index/P80000912.htm

Supporters:
Al Gore for President 2000
http://www.perkel.com/politics/clinton/gore.htm

Disabled Friends of Al Gore
http://www.disabledforgore.org/

Veterans for Al Gore 2000
http://members.aol.com/vetschoice/ag2000.htm

Dirty Laundry:
Al Gore Skeleton Closet
http://www.realchange.org/gore.htm

Parodies:
Bore 2000
http://www.albore.com/

Affiliated Organizations:
Office of the Vice President of the U.S.
http://www.whitehouse.gov/WH/EOP/OVP/index-plain.html

PAC Finance Data:
Center for Responsive Politics
http://www.opensecrets.org/pacs/pacgot/00165753.htm

FECInfo
http://www.tray.com/cgi-win/_pacwhere.exe?C00165753

Orrin G. Hatch

Hatch was elected to the U.S. Senate from Utah in 1976 and reelected in 1982, 1988, and 1994. Before his election to the Senate, he practiced law. He is affiliated with a leadership PAC, Capitol Committee. Hatch announced the formation of an exploratory committee to consider a bid for the Republican nomination for president on July 1, 1999.

Websites

Official Campaign Headquarters:
President Orrin Hatch
http://www.orrinhatch.org/

Campaign Finance Data:
Center for Responsive Politics
http://www.opensecrets.org/politicians/index/
S6UT00063.htm

Supporters:
Orrin Hatch for President
http://www.newpioneer.org/hatch01.htm

Dirty Laundry: —

Parodies: —

Affiliated Organizations:
U.S. Senate Office
http://www.senate.gov/~hatch/

PAC Finance Data:
Center for Responsive Politics
http://www.opensecrets.org/pacs/pacgot/
00235572.htm

FECInfo
http://www.tray.com/cgi-win/_pacwhere.exe?
C00235572

John R. Kasich

Kasich has served in Congress as a representative from Ohio since 1983. Before that he served in the Ohio state legislature. He is affiliated with a leadership PAC, Pioneer PAC, and a state PAC in New Hampshire by the same name. Kasich announced the formation of an exploratory committee to consider a bid for the Republican nomination for president on February 15, 1999. He dropped out of the race on July 14, 1999, endorsing George W. Bush Jr.

Websites

Official Campaign Headquarters:
John Kasich 2000
http://www.k2k.org/

Campaign Finance Data:
Center for Responsive Politics
http://www.opensecrets.org/politicians/index/
H2OH12027.htm

Supporters:
Kasich 2000
http://www.kasich2000.org/

The John Kasich FanClub
http://members.aol.com/kasichfan1/

The Unofficial Utah K2K
http://www.vii.com/~pchcty/k2k/

Dirty Laundry: —

Parodies: —

Affiliated Organizations:
U.S. House Office
http://www.house.gov/kasich/

Pioneer PAC
http://www.pioneerpac.org/

PAC Finance Data:
Center for Responsive Politics
http://www.opensecrets.org/pacs/pacgot/
00325357.htm

FECInfo
http://www.tray.com/cgi-win/_pacwhere.exe?
C00325357

State of New Hampshire
http://www.state.nh.us/sos/filings/

Alan L. Keyes

Keyes served as U.S. ambassador to the United Nations and as assistant secretary of state for President Ronald Reagan. In 1988 and 1992 he ran unsuccessfully for the Senate. He also ran an unsuccessful campaign for the Republican nomination for president in 1996. Keyes has been a nationally syndicated radio talk show host and is chair of the federal PAC, Black America's Political Action Committee (BAMPAC). Keyes formed an exploratory committee to consider a bid for the Republican nomination for president on June 17, 1999.

Websites

Official Campaign Headquarters:
Keyes 2000
http://www.keyes2000.org/

Campaign Finance Data: —

Supporters:
Keyes 2000 - North Dakota
http://www.dakotaprairie.com/keyes/

Dirty Laundry:
Alan Keyes Skeleton Closet
http://www.realchange.org/keyes.htm

Parodies: —

Affiliated Organizations:
BAMPAC
http://www.bampac.org/

The Alan Keyes Show
http://alankeyes.com/

PAC Finance Data:
Center for Responsive Politics
http://www.opensecrets.org/pacs/pacgot/
00300921.htm

John S. McCain III

McCain served in the U.S. Navy from 1958 through 1981. In 1967 he was shot down over North Vietnam and was held as a prisoner of war for five and a half years. He served in Congress from 1983 through 1987 as a representative from Arizona. In 1986 he was elected to the U.S. Senate from Arizona and was reelected in 1992 and 1998. McCain announced the formation of an exploratory committee to pursue a bid for the Republican nomination for president on April 13, 1999.

Websites

Official Campaign Headquarters:
McCain 2000
http://www.mccain2000.com/

McCain 2000 interactive
http://www.mccaininteractive.com/

It's Your Country
http://www.itsyourcountry.com/

Campaign Finance Data:
Center for Responsive Politics
http://www.opensecrets.org/2000elect/index/
P80002801.htm

Supporters: —

Dirty Laundry:
John McCain Skeleton Closet
http://www.realchange.org/mccain.htm

Parodies:
Phoenix New Times: "Running John"
http://www.phoenixnewtimes.com/extra/
running_john/

Affiliated Organizations:
U.S. Senate Office
http://www.senate.gov/~mccain/

PAC Finance Data: —

Ralph Nader

Nader is a consumer and liberal reform activist. In 1996 he ran for president as the Green Party nominee, receiving almost 700,000 votes. He has told the Green Party that he may run for president again in 2000 but will not make a decision until early 2000.

Websites

Official Campaign Headquarters: —

Campaign Finance Data: —

Supporters:
The Nader Page
http://www.nader.org/

Dirty Laundry:
Ralph Nader Skeleton Closet
http://www.realchange.org/nader.htm

Parodies: —

Affiliated Organizations:
The Association of State Green Parties
http://www.greenparties.org/

Green Party USA
http://www.greens.org/gpusa/

PAC Finance Data: —

H. Ross Perot

Perot is a billionaire businessman who is CEO of Perot Systems. He was an independent nominee for president in 1992 and the nominee of the Reform Party, which he helped to found, in 1996. In both elections, he received record levels of support for a third-party or independent presidential candidate. Although he has been loath to discuss his electoral plans for 2000, the public's dissatisfaction with either the Democratic or Republican nominee (or both) may tempt Perot to pursue a third campaign for president.

Websites

Official Campaign Headquarters:
Ross Perot—Official World Wide Web Site
http://www.perot.org/

Campaign Finance Data: —

Supporters:
Perot 2000
http://members.aol.com/DukeofRush/index.html

Texans for Perot
http://www.soft-vision.com/perot/

Dirty Laundry:
Ross Perot Skeleton Closet
http://www.realchange.org/perot.htm

Parodies:
The Daily Muse
http://www.cais.net/aschnedr//perot.htm

Affiliated Organizations:
Perot Systems
http://www.perotsystems.com/index.asp

Reform Party
http://www.reformparty.org/

PAC Finance Data: —

J. Danforth Quayle

Quayle served in Congress from 1976 through 1980 as a representative from Indiana. In 1980 he was elected to the U.S. Senate from Indiana and reelected in 1986. He was elected vice president in 1988, with George Bush as president, and defeated for reelection in 1992. Quayle is associated with a leadership PAC, Campaign America, and two state PACs in New Hampshire and Virginia by the same name. He declared his candidacy for the Republican nomination for president on April 14, 1999.

Websites

Official Campaign Headquarters:
Dan Quayle for President Committee
http://www.quayle.org/

Campaign Finance Data:
Center for Responsive Politics
http://www.opensecrets.org/2000elect/index/P80002587.htm

Supporters: —

Dirty Laundry:
Dan Quayle Skeleton Closet
http://www.realchange.org/quayle.htm

Parodies:
Dan Quayle For Pope in 2000
http://www.spiny.com/pope/

Affiliated Organizations:
The Dan Quayle Center and Museum
http://www.quaylemuseum.org/

PAC Finance Data:
Center for Responsive Politics
http://www.opensecrets.org/pacs/pacgot/00088369.htm

http://www.opensecrets.org/pacs/vadata.htm

FECInfo
http://www.tray.com/cgi-win/_pacwhere.exe?C00088369

State of New Hampshire
http://www.state.nh.us/sos/filings/

Robert C. "Bob" Smith

Smith was elected to the U.S. Senate from New Hampshire in 1990 and was reelected in 1996. Before that, he served as a representative from New Hampshire. He is affiliated with the Live Free or Die PAC. Smith announced his candidacy for the Republican nomination for president on February 18, 1999. On July 13, 1999, however, he declared that he would leave the Republican Party and seek the nomination for president as an independent or member of a third party.

Websites

Official Campaign Headquarters:
Bob Smith for President
http://www.smithforpresident.org/

Campaign Finance Data:
  Center for Responsive Politics
  http://www.opensecrets.org/2000elect/index/
  P00003376.htm

Supporters: —

Dirty Laundry: —

Parodies: —

Affiliated Organizations:
  U.S. Senate Office
  http://www.senate.gov/~smith/

PAC Finance Data:
  Center for Responsive Politics
  http://www.opensecrets.org/pacs/pacgot/
  00330134.htm

  FECInfo
  http://www.tray.com/cgi-win/_pacwhere.exe?
  C00330134

"Jesse Ventura" (James Janos)

Ventura was elected governor of Minnesota in 1998. He is also a former mayor of Brooklyn Park, Minnesota. Before that, he served in the U.S. Navy, pursued a successful career in professional wrestling, and was a radio talk show host. Although Ventura has said he is not a candidate for president in 2000, his prominence as the first and only Reform Party candidate to win statewide office may eventually prompt him to declare his candidacy.

Websites

Official Campaign Headquarters: —

Campaign Finance Data: —

Supporters:
  The Jesse Ventura Store Online
  http://www.cottageindustry.com/jesse/

  Jesse Watch
  http://politicsonline.com/jv/

  The Ventura Files
  http://www.venturafiles.com/

  Draft Jesse Ventura for President Committee
  http://www.presidentventura.com/

  Ventura Citizen Action Committee
  http://www.dreamagic.com/jesse.html

Dirty Laundry: —

Parodies:
  King Jesse's Jesters
  http://www.kingjessesjesters.com/

Affiliated Organizations:
  Office of the Minnesota Governor
  http://www.mainserver.state.mn.us/governor/

  Jesse Ventura Volunteer Committee
  http://www.jesseventura.org/

  Reform Party
  http://www.reformparty.org/

PAC Finance Data: —

Index

Page references followed by *t, f,* or *b* indicate tables, figures, or boxes, respectively.